Shadowing Multilingual Learners

Second Edition

Shadowing Multilingual Learners

Second Edition

Ivannia Soto

The Education Trust-West Promising Practice

FOR INFORMATION:

Corwin

A SAGE Company

2455 Teller Road

Thousand Oaks, California 91320

(800) 233-9936

www.corwin.com

SAGE Publications Ltd.

1 Oliver's Yard

55 City Road

London EC1Y 1SP

United Kingdom

SAGE Publications India Pvt. Ltd.

B 1/I 1 Mohan Cooperative Industrial Area

Mathura Road, New Delhi 110 044

India

SAGE Publications Asia-Pacific Pte. Ltd.

18 Cross Street #10-10/11/12

China Square Central

Singapore 048423

Program Director and Publisher: Dan Alpert

Senior Content Development Editor: Lucas Schleicher

Associate Content Development Editor: Mia Rodriguez

Production Editor: Megha Negi

Copy Editor: Kim Husband

Typesetter: C&M Digitals (P) Ltd.

Proofreader: Talia Greenberg

Indexer: Integra

Cover Designer: Karine Hovsepian

Marketing Manager: Maura Sullivan

Library of Congress Cataloging-in-Publication Data

Names: Soto, Ivannia, author.

Title: Shadowing multilingual learners / Ivannia Soto.

Other titles: ELL shadowing as a catalyst for change

Description: Second edition. | Thousand Oaks, California : Corwin, [2021] | Series: Corwin literacy | "Previous edition title, ELL shadowing as a catalyst for change, c2012." | Includes bibliographical references and index.

Identifiers: LCCN 2020046686 | ISBN 9781071818589 (paperback) | ISBN 9781071818596 (epub) | ISBN 9781071818602 (epub) | ISBN 9781071818626 (pdf)

Subjects: LCSH: Linguistic minorities—Education—United States. | Children with social disabilities—Education—United States. | Language arts—Remedial teaching—United States. | Individualized instruction—United States. | Observation (Educational method)

Classification: LCC LC3731 .S666 2021 | DDC 370.1170973—dc23

LC record available at https://lccn.loc.gov/2020046686

This book is printed on acid-free paper.

SUSTAINABLE FORESTRY INITIATIVE

Certified Chain of Custody

Promoting Sustainable Forestry

www.sfiprogram.org

SFI-01268

21 22 23 24 25 10 9 8 7 6 5 4 3 2 1

Contents

Visit the companion website at
http://resources.corwin.com/shadowingmultilinguallearners
for downloadable resources.

Visit
https://www.whittier.edu/iclrt/resources
for video resources

Acknowledgments

It has now been 10 years since the first edition of this book was published and 14 years since we conducted the first MLL shadowing project in the Los Angeles Unified School District (LAUSD). Since that first shadowing project in 2003, this process has been used across California, in almost every county office of education, as well as many school districts across the state. MLL shadowing projects have also been conducted across the country in New York, New Mexico, and Illinois. In 2016, the MLL Shadowing app was developed, creating what I now call MLL Shadowing 2.0. Special thanks to the California Community Foundation for a generous grant to assist with developing the app and to Linda Meyer for programming the app. Lastly, one of the major highlights on this journey of MLL shadowing was in 2018, when Education Trust-West recognized MLL shadowing as a promising practice for MLLs. I am grateful for what each of those shadowing projects taught me: to be persistent and determined to continue to advocate for this group of students.

I am still indebted to Dr. Linda J. Carstens, who was integral in developing the multilingual learner (MLL) shadowing process. This book came out of an innovative and magical time for professional learning and development in District 6 of LAUSD. A variety of district office members, including Dr. Dale Vigil, Glynn Thompson, Edward Manson, Cindy Paulos, and David Manzo, helped lead the effort. I am grateful to have been able to work with and learn so much from each of you during that time in my life.

What's New in This Edition

There are five major additions included in the second edition of this book. In the first chapter, I discuss the reason behind the change in the title of the book. Here, I will explain the five major additions as follows.

- **Lessons learned:** I have been conducting shadowing projects both in California and nationally since 2003. Along the way, there have been many lessons learned, especially when working with school districts on shadowing projects over time. In this edition of the book, I add additional examples of work with school districts, county offices, and bilingual resource networks between 2012 and 2021. Many of the systemic resources for multilingual success that were developed as I worked hand in hand with school systems are included. These resources are both embedded in the chapters and in the appendices.

- **New strategy resources:** Chapter 10 has been revamped to include all three academic language development strategies proposed after the initial shadowing training. Specifically, the Frayer model and resources for how to use the Frayer model with multilingual students have been added. Additional tools and resources for further scaffolding of Think-Pair-Share have also been included.

- **Shadowing in a virtual setting:** Multiple chapters address how to shadow in a virtual setting. Specifically, there are four ways proposed to use shadowing in a virtual setting, including:

  1. Using videos, such as the following from Jeff Zwiers: https://jeffzwiers .org/videos. Please note that these videos are exemplars. Teachers can select one student per video to shadow and use the beginning and end of each video as a time stamp for shadowing;

  2. Teachers can shadow in a breakout session by identifying a multilingual learner and shadowing them in this small-group setting;

3. Teachers can record their own teaching via Zoom and then go back and view the video to shadow a multilingual student in their own classroom;

4. Administrators can request a substitute teacher so that the teacher of record can shadow in another classroom.

- **Shadowing in multilingual settings:** Shadowing was done extensively for 2 years in dual-language immersion (DLI) settings, and the process has been added to this edition of the book. Shadowing in DLI settings can focus on determining if there are equitable learning environments for multilingual learners in these programs. Additionally, language allocation models can be monitored using shadowing. Lastly, shadowing in multilingual settings can assist educators with experiencing the benefits of biliteracy programs.

- **Shadowing app:** This edition of the book includes information on the development of the Multilingual Shadowing app, which was piloted for 2 years and is available for use through the author. Included is a step-by-step process that describes how to use the app, as well as how the app differs from the paper–pencil version of the protocol.

About the Author

Dr. Ivannia Soto is Professor of Education and Director of Graduate Programs at Whittier College, where she specializes in second-language acquisition, systemic reform for English language learners (ELLs), and urban education. She began her career in the Los Angeles Unified School District (LAUSD), where she taught English and English language development to a population made up of 99.9% Latinos, who either were or had been MLLs. Before becoming a professor, Dr. Soto also served LAUSD as a literacy coach and district office administrator. She has presented on literacy and language topics at various conferences, including the National Association for Bilingual Education (NABE), the California Association for Bilingual Association (CABE), the American Educational Research Association (AERA), and the National Urban Education Conference. As a consultant, Soto has worked with Stanford University's School Redesign Network (SRN), WestEd, and CABE, as well as a variety of districts and county offices in California, providing technical assistance for systemic reform for MLLs and Title III. Soto has authored and co-authored 13 books, including *The Literacy Gaps: Building Bridges for MLLs and SELs*; *MLL Shadowing as a Catalyst for Change*, which was recognized by Education Trust-West as a promising practice for MLLs in 2018; *From Spoken to Written Language with MLLs*; the *Academic English Mastery* four-book series; the *ELD Companion* series; *Breaking Down the Wall*; and *Responsive Schooling for Culturally and Linguistically Diverse Students*. Together, the books tell a story of how to systemically close achievement gaps with MLLs by increasing their academic language production across content areas. Soto is executive director of the Institute for Culturally and Linguistically Responsive Teaching (ICLRT) at Whittier College, whose mission it is to promote relevant research and develop academic resources for MLLs and standard English learners (SELs) via linguistically and culturally responsive teaching practices.

Introduction

My parents, Blanca Estela Artavia Soto and Rodrigo Soto, immigrated to the United States from Costa Rica—my mother when she was 11 years old and my father when he was 21 years old. Their story, like that of many children of immigrants, is central to my work with schools and in teacher education, as well as to my research passions now as an adult. My mother went to school in LAUSD during a time when a systemic plan for working with multilingual learners (MLLs) was uncharted territory. Although she spent many more years in United States schools than in Costa Rican schools, in high school, she quickly noticed that she was not developing the English language skills that she would need to become proficient. Being the self-starter that she was (and still is), my mother became her own advocate and enrolled herself in additional adult-school English classes in order to receive the English language instruction that she needed and deserved. It is because of her persistence and determination that my sister, Arlene Soto Smith, and I have furthered ourselves in this country as we have.

Unfortunately, this notion of not systemically meeting the instructional needs of our MLLs still exists today. Although we now have a strong body of research literature pointing toward best practices with MLLs—which includes dual-language education—and even though we have more and more district, state, and federal policies in place to meet the instructional needs of MLLs, the same inequities that my mother contended with more than 51 years ago continue to prevail. Such imbalances fuel my work. When I review data and see that opportunity gaps still exist, read articles about the politics of why we are not educationally advancing the way we need to, or work with districts that are in state sanction because they are not making adequate yearly progress with their MLLs, I refuse to stop trying to create change within systems. Part of the reason is when I see all of these issues in education, I see them through the lens of one person—my mother—and that keeps me going. That is the purpose of MLL shadowing—reflecting upon a day in the life of a child or adolescent multilanguage learner who brings a plethora of linguistic and cultural assets to school.

Throughout this book, you will get to know one MLL named Josue. Although he is a compilation of all of the MLLs that I have shadowed, he represents the invisibility and silence that many of our MLLs experience in school. But Josue, like my mother before him, has a story; he must be allowed to gain voice and an academic identity in the classroom setting. He needs to be engaged and heard and understood in the classroom. He has so much to say if we would only elicit his speech and listen. . . . Remember Josue each time you use this book. You will never teach the same way again—I promise.

SECTION I

Purpose of Shadowing

CHAPTER 1

Creating a Sense of Urgency

One of the major revisions that has been made to the second edition of this book, which you might have already noticed, is the use of *multilingual learner (MLL)* instead of *English language learner* (please note that some scholars use *emergent bilinguals*, but MLLs was selected for this book to honor students for whom English is their third or fourth language). This shift was intended to create an urgency for change at a time when the language and labels that we use matter more than ever. The shift in what we call multilingual students can and will impact our perspectives and our expectations of them, including their achievement, language usage, and academic identities in the classroom setting. When we begin to use assets-based language and move away from monolingual deficit-based labels, we will begin to view multilingualism as a resource and something that must be built upon. This modification in language labels necessitates a shift in mindset regarding what we believe and are expecting to see multilinguals achieve in the classroom setting. Instead of only hearing and accepting English in classroom spaces, it is essential that we view their primary language as an asset not only as a means to obtain proficiency in English but also for its own merit and contribution to biliteracy, bilingualism, and sociocultural competence. As Valdés (2010, p. 1) suggests in her testimony before the U.S. Equal Employment Opportunity Commission,

> Bilingual individuals, whether they are circumstantial [the conquered, colonized, displaced] or elective [electing to learn a foreign language used for travel or other purpose], are never two monolinguals in one person (Grosjean, 1989, 1998, 2010). Their

language development and acquisition reflects the opportunities that they have to interact with individuals who speak those languages. More importantly perhaps circumstantial bilinguals become bilingual as part of bilingual communities. In the United States these communities include (1) newly arrived monolinguals that speak a non-English language, (2) a large number of persons who have varying strengths in both English and a non-English language and (3) established third generation individuals of their same ethnic group who may now be English-speaking monolinguals. Bilinguals communicate on a daily basis using bilingual communicative strategies most recently referred to as translanguaging (Creese & Blackledge, 2005). This means that they use the linguistic resources of one or both of their languages to communicate most effectively. Rather than using a six-string guitar, when bilinguals speak to other bilinguals they use a twelve-string guitar using communicative strategies. They do not have to limit themselves to a single language to express nuanced messages.

Imagine if we indeed believed that all of our MLLs brought the ability to use a twelve-string guitar, instead of a six-string guitar, to the classroom setting! How might our classroom change? How might our expectations and belief systems change? How might our ability to view these linguistic gifts help us to build not only classroom bridges but societal bridges? As we shadow students by keeping this assets-based mental model in mind, I invite you to look for all of the linguistic and cultural gifts that your MLLs bring to school.

FOUR ESSENTIAL SHIFTS EDUCATORS MUST MAKE ON BEHALF OF MULTILINGUAL LEARNERS

A lot has been written about the essential shifts that are needed for native English-speaking students when the Common Core State Standards movement emerged, but not much has been written or addressed about those essential shifts for MLLs. As such, the four essential shifts that educators must make on behalf of their MLLs include:

1. Language development across the curriculum;

2. Use of rigorous and complex texts and content with appropriate scaffolding;

3. Increased focus on oral language and multiple opportunities for speaking and listening;

4. Emphasis on inquiry, collaboration, and teamwork.

Notice that each of these essential shifts necessitates having and holding high expectations on behalf of MLLs. If we do not have high expectations, we would not infuse language development across the curriculum; nor would we use rigorous and complex texts with appropriate scaffolding. If we do not hold high expectations, we would not believe in student-centered classrooms where students do the thinking, talking, and heavy lifting in pairs and small groups. What follows is the unpacking of what the essential shifts mean for MLLs in the classroom setting.

Language development across the curriculum refers to the notion that language should be central to all academic subject areas. This means that all teachers are teachers of language, and they must know how language intersects with their discipline. Language is what all subject areas have in common, and for MLLs, it is the hidden curriculum of how to unpack content.

FIGURE 1.1   Language Is Central to All Academic Areas

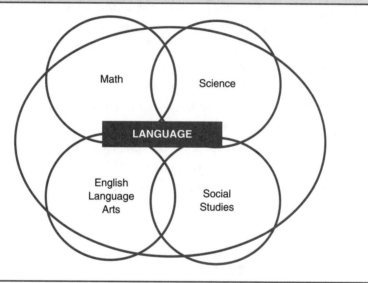

By explicitly teaching the essential elements of language within each content area, we are providing an essential scaffold that MLLs need to succeed. The essential elements of academic language include register, academic vocabulary, syntax, and grammar (Kinsella, 2007). The academic language development strategies outlined in the second part of this book are directly aligned with these essential components of academic language. The register of language refers to MLLs using the appropriate language set for the context that they find themselves in, either social or academic. Explicitly teaching the register of language does not mean that we want to take away a primary language or variation of English. Instead, it means that students have the ability to code switch and use different registers of language, as needed. Oftentimes, MLLs are relegated to basic, Tier 1 vocabulary instead of high-utility words (Tier 2) and discipline-specific words (Tier 3). MLLs need a full diet of academic vocabulary that is taught in a contextualized manner. In order to embrace multilingualism, teachers must teach and explicitly address cognates (words that sound alike and have similar meanings in two languages) so as to honor the conceptual knowledge that MLLs bring to school and merely add a new linguistic label in English. Grammar and syntax should also be taught in a contextualized way. In order for MLLs to access rigorous content, they must be taught grammar and syntax in context to the texts and writing assignments that they are engaged in. MLLs also need to be taught how syntactical and grammatical concepts are different between English and their primary language by using contrastive analysis.

We cannot and must not rest until every group of students receives the kind of education inherent in the four shifts listed earlier. This book will remind the reader of a group currently struggling with inequity within the U.S. educational system: MLLs. It will also propose a way to create systemic urgency for this group of students, using both processes for change and an ethnographic research method called MLL shadowing. MLL shadowing is a professional-development design that involves a single teacher observing a single MLL during the course of a school day (or at minimum 2 hours). I often describe the process as experiencing a day in the life of an MLL by taking a snapshot of his or her speaking and active listening experiences at the start of every 5 minutes over the course of 2 hours. This process becomes a powerful way to shed light on the specific linguistic and cultural needs of MLLs. MLL shadowing, in conjunction with follow-up professional development, allows educators to begin to create systemic instructional access and equity for MLLs.

PREPARING TEACHERS TO INSTRUCT MULTILINGUAL LEARNERS

Teachers go into teaching with good intentions. But somehow, the demands of the classroom—sometimes the size, the lack of resources, or the variability in language ability level—begin to wear on educators. These demands are coupled with the fact that teacher education and preservice programs are not doing enough to train teachers to meet the linguistic and cultural needs of this very specific student population (Wei, Darling-Hammond, Andree, Richardson, & Orphanos, 2009). California, for example, with its surge in MLL numbers, has moved toward an embedded certification process, requiring, in most colleges and universities, one course that addresses the needs of MLLs while also integrating topics focusing on MLLs into the rest of the teacher-preparation coursework. In other words, teachers in California come out of teacher-preparation programs with an embedded MLL certification as part of their overall credentialing process. While this looks like a positive concept at the outset because all teachers become certified to teach MLLs, teachers no longer have to take additional coursework outside of their credentials to teach MLLs. Although every teacher is required to complete minimal coursework to teach MLLs, this is hardly enough to become effective with the specific needs of MLLs or the demands that teachers experience in the field once they are required to teach them. Although California is unique in this approach to preparing mainstream teachers to teach MLLs, the fact that the majority of states do not require such certification also demonstrates a need for focused and ongoing professional development on the specific needs of this group of students. Both preservice and inservice training about the needs of MLLs is needed to create systemic instructional and achievement change.

FOCUSED AND ONGOING PROFESSIONAL DEVELOPMENT ON MLLs

In addition to preservice training, teachers also need focused, sustained, and aligned professional development once they enter the field. If preservice teachers are receiving only one course focused on the needs of MLLs, and others receive no such course at all, then all teachers need additional opportunities to refine their scaffolding skills with MLLs once they enter the teaching field. According to findings from Learning Forward (formerly known as the National Staff Development Council), "Teachers are not getting adequate training in teaching special education or limited English proficiency students. More than two-thirds of teachers nationally had not had even one day of training in supporting the learning of special education or LEP [MLL] students during the previous three years" (Wei et al., 2009, p. 6). Specifically, teachers would benefit from both a series of courses and a variety of coursework experiences that sensitize them to meet the specific linguistic and cultural needs of MLLs in our schools. Additionally, when teachers enter their classrooms, ongoing and focused professional development that supports them in best meeting the needs of MLLs and scaffolding instruction for this group of students is paramount to closing students' literacy gaps (Soto-Hinman & Hetzel, 2009). Learning Forward also suggests that teachers need close to 50 hours of professional development to improve their skills and their students' learning. This means that teacher learning must also be ongoing. Professional development must be focused, aligned, and coherent. It should not change from year to year or when the new flavor of the month appears. Teachers need time to become skilled at practices that will improve student achievement. Professional development should also be data driven, connected to the specific needs of students at a school site, and therefore personalized.

As Darling-Hammond (2009, p. 30) suggests,

> Teacher qualifications, teachers' knowledge and skills, make more difference for student learning than any other single factor. Clearly, this means that if we want to improve student learning, what we

have to do is invest in teachers' learning. We have to be sure that teachers understand not only their content area, which is very important, but also, how do students learn? How do different students learn differently? How do students acquire language? How do second language learners need to be taught?

In this way, both preservice and inservice training must become more focused and aligned in both the course work and field work opportunities required, in order to ensure appropriate cultural and linguistic differentiation for MLLs. The MLL shadowing project is one way to provide a focused and sustained effort around the academic speaking and listening needs of MLLs within a system.

WHAT IS THE MLL SHADOWING PROJECT?

The MLL shadowing project is a way to create urgency around the instructional and linguistic needs of MLLs, either in teacher training or in staff development. The process allows teachers to see firsthand, in classrooms that look like their own, the sense of urgency that exists when the specific needs of MLLs are not addressed systemically. There are different kinds of MLLs—newcomers who are highly literate, educated, or underschooled; long-term MLLs who have been in the country 6 years or longer; and MLLs progressing predictably through the developmental sequence. It is imperative to tailor professional development and instruction to the specific needs of MLLs at a school site (Olsen, 2006). With the MLL shadowing project, this means that if most MLLs at a particular school or district lie at the midrange of English language proficiency, students at that level of language progression should be tracked for the MLL shadowing experience. This will allow the system to draw attention to the particular level of proficiency needed while encouraging everyone to focus on that one specific group for a particular period of time. Inversely, if a range of MLLs is represented within a system, then each shadower can select a student at a different proficiency level and then compare results during the debrief session. Educators will then also be able to target follow-up professional-development sessions and focus on instructional strategies for that specific group or groups of MLLs. The time of random acts of scaffolding usage should be gone, and we must instead tailor instruction to data collected on gaps in instruction. The MLL shadowing project is a way to triangulate achievement data with classroom observations to better serve the academic needs of MLLs.

The MLL shadowing project also allows all teachers within a system—whether it be grade level or department, entire school, district, or county office—to focus on the specific needs of an MLL through the lens of one student. Systems often do not get the opportunity to reflect on their practices and focus their efforts in one direction. The MLL shadowing project is an opportunity to do so over a 3-day period to begin a new systemic vision for change with this group of students.

Additionally, the MLL shadowing project allows professional development to be focused and directed to the specific needs of the MLL population being served within a system. Since specific classroom data on academic speaking and listening are collected through the MLL shadowing project, subsequent professional development can be differentiated and tailored so that the academic needs of MLLs within that particular system are met. In most districts and schools across the country, the needs of MLL populations are expansive, so the professional development and focus on this population of students must also be ongoing to properly address those needs. MLL shadowing is not a panacea, so there must be follow-up training on how to address the linguistic and cultural needs of this population of students in order that MLLs begin to make the kind of progress needed to become multilingual.

MLL Shadowing for Progress Monitoring

MLL shadowing can also be used regularly for progress monitoring when awareness has been created around a certain group at a particular level. There are a variety of ways to utilize MLL shadowing for progress monitoring once first-year, baseline data have been collected. First, once follow-up professional development has been provided around the three academic language development strategies outlined in Chapter 10, systems can shadow the same students again to see if the percentage of student talk has increased. Many districts, including Anaheim Union High School District (AUHSD) in Southern California, have set districtwide and/or schoolwide goals for classroom talk. After conducting shadowing projects in their first year, AUHSD decided to set a districtwide goal of 30% student talk in the classroom setting. Shadowing was then conducted again in year 2 in order to determine if they had met that goal or needed to provide additional professional development.

Second, once follow-up professional development has been provided for teachers on how to create more academic speaking in the classroom setting, teachers can visit each other's classrooms in order to monitor and learn from student engagement strategies being used. If professional development has been offered around incorporating productive group work structures, teachers can visit each other's classrooms to learn from colleagues to determine if the amount of listening and speaking has increased by using specific academic oral language development instructional strategies. In this way, MLL shadowing can be used alongside existing professional-development structures, including instructional coaching models, professional learning communities (PLCs), Response to Intervention (RTI), or Sheltered Instruction Observation Protocol (SIOP). The MLL shadowing project can enhance and accompany other initiatives by placing a spotlight on the needs of MLLs within a system. Once specific needs have been determined for MLLs using the shadowing experience, existing structures that are in place can be used alongside the initiative to assist with sustaining instructional change. If existing structures are currently not in place, there are suggestions for creating such structures in Chapter 10 of this book.

What MLL Shadowing Is Not

It is important to note that MLL shadowing is not intended to be the be-all and end-all—it is not a panacea or a silver bullet. MLL shadowing is the beginning of awareness and focus on the specific academic assets and needs of MLLs, but educators often don't view their classrooms and students in the same way after having had the experience. After an MLL shadowing training in Lucia Mar Unified School District in Arroyo Grande, California, where 90 teachers and administrators were in attendance, educators reflected in their evaluation of the training with comments like, "I will never look at classroom instruction the same again," and "This is the most powerful professional development I have ever been through," as well as, "I think that shadowing should be done every year to reflect on our teaching" (confidential training evaluations, 2010).

Still, the MLL shadowing project is only the first step in creating systemic achievement and instructional change for MLLs within a system. Once the MLL shadowing project itself has been completed, ongoing and sustained follow-up professional development must also be provided so that teachers then know *how* to change instructional practices in their classrooms for MLLs. As suggested earlier, 50 hours of sustained and consistent professional development over time are needed in order to begin to change teacher practice (Wei et al., 2009). This book contributes to teacher development by providing (1) ways of shadowing an MLL in order to create urgency and (2) specific instructional strategies to change systemic practices and scaffold instruction via academic language development techniques once MLL shadowing has been completed.

ORGANIZATION OF THE BOOK

Throughout the book, we follow one MLL student named Josue. Although a pseudonym has been used, Josue is a compilation of many MLLs that I have shadowed since 2003, when shadowing was first developed. Chapter 2 introduces the history and context of MLL shadowing, with its inception in the Los Angeles Unified School District's (LAUSD) Local District 6. Chapter 3 provides a mini case study about Josue with specific emphasis on the classroom observation of this MLL. Josue's achievement results have been included both in Chapter 3 and in Chapter 6. We also follow Josue's progress in listening and academic speaking throughout several chapters (academic speaking in Chapters 4 and 7 and academic listening in Chapters 5 and 7). You will find some redundancy in the book. That is intentional in order to ensure a clear understanding of how to complete the MLL shadowing project. In this way, Chapter 4 provides the research base for academic speaking but also introduces how to use the MLL shadowing protocol for academic speaking specifically. Similarly, in Chapter 5, the reader is introduced to the importance of teaching academic listening explicitly as well as how to use the protocol for listening specifically. Chapter 6 presents an overview of the logistics of setting up an MLL shadowing training in a school, district, or county. In Chapter 7, the reader will find a detailed overview of how to use all portions of the MLL shadowing protocol to ensure that the process is adhered to with fidelity. Chapter 8 discusses how to analyze results from an MLL shadowing project, and Chapter 9 introduces how a system might leverage change based on the MLL shadowing experience. Finally, Chapter 10 discusses what to do after the MLL shadowing experience, including strategy suggestions for ways to elicit more academic speaking and active listening in a classroom setting. The accompanying online video clips present classroom teachers in diverse classrooms implementing Think-Pair-Share for listening and speaking, reciprocal teaching for listening and speaking, and the Frayer Model for vocabulary development.

This book is also primarily based on the text *Scaffolding Language, Scaffolding Learning*, by Pauline Gibbons (2002), in which she discusses how to scaffold the literacy domains of speaking, listening, reading, and writing with MLLs. The MLL shadowing experience is primarily based on the speaking (Chapter 2) and listening (Chapter 6) chapters of Gibbons's text, as these are the two domains that educators will monitor when they engage in shadowing. These are also often the two most undertaught and underdeveloped domains of language, even though speaking is a scaffold for writing and listening is a scaffold for reading. Although other literature has been cited, the MLL shadowing project was created as a culminating experience after a book study on the Gibbons text in 2003 in District 6 of the LAUSD. More about the historical context of MLL shadowing can be read in Chapter 3.

This book is not intended to be the only source for reading on the importance of academic speaking and listening with MLLs. Additional study groups during PLCs or department or grade-level meetings can be formed after the MLL shadowing project in order to extend knowledge of academic speaking and active listening. Similarly, the academic oral language development definition and instructional strategies outlined in Chapter 10 are starting points for systemic change, but they are not intended to be the only definition or strategies used.

As you read about Josue throughout this book, think about an MLL in your own classroom. When you shadow an MLL, think about what you might do differently in your own classroom the very next day. Being reflective about what you do every day to scaffold instruction for MLLs will assist not only in addressing opportunity gaps but also in creating instructional access for MLLs in their academic futures. You will then become a part of creating an urgency for change on behalf of MLLs.

REFERENCES

Darling-Hammond, L. (2009). *Linda Darling-Hammond: Thoughts on teacher preparation*. Retrieved from http://www.edutopia.org/ldh-teacher-preparation

Gibbons, P. (2002). *Scaffolding language, scaffolding learning: Teacher second language learners in the mainstream classroom*. Portsmouth, NH: Heinemann.

Kinsella, K. (2007). *Bolstering academic language and reading comprehension*. Power-Point presentation at the Academic Language Development Workshop, Mountain View School, El Monte, CA. Available at http://www.sccoe.k12.ca.us/depts/MLL/kinsMLLa_2009.asp

Olsen, L. (2006). Ensuring academic success for English learners. *University of California Linguistic Minority Research Institute Newsletter, 15*(4), 1–7.

Soto-Hinman, I., & Hetzel, J. (2009). *The literacy gaps: Building bridges for English language learners and standard English learners*. Thousand Oaks, CA: Corwin.

Valdés, G. (2010). *Written testimony to the members of the U.S. Equal Employment Opportunity Commission Select Task Force on the Study of Harassment in the Workplace*. Washington, D.C.: U.S. Equal Employment Opportunity Commission.

Wei, R. C., Darling-Hammond, L., Andree, A., Richardson, N., & Orphanos, S. (2009). *Professional learning in the learning profession: A status report on teacher development in the United States and abroad*. Dallas, TX: National Staff Development Council.

CHAPTER 2

History and Context of Shadowing

The power of multilingual learner (MLL) shadowing is in the student. As educators within educational systems, we do not often have the opportunity to observe one student and experience instruction from that student's perspective. In this manner, the power of MLL shadowing is in the opportunity to come together as a system to observe the needs of MLLs through the same lens and then have the opportunity to discuss what was viewed from the standpoint of one MLL. MLL shadowing is a catalyst by which all educators within a system can align and become clearer around the specific needs of MLLs within their particular context or setting, whether it is at a school site, within a district, or at the county level. Usually, we go into classrooms to observe or evaluate teachers. The purpose of MLL shadowing is to observe a day in the instructional life of one MLL. When you go into a classroom filled to the brim with 30 students, it is easy to place blame or be overwhelmed by the sheer numbers. When you look at the instructional needs of one student at a time, it is difficult to turn away. As educators, we become connected again, and the reasons why we went into education are realized anew.

The first MLL shadowing project was conducted in 2003 in Local District 6 of the Los Angeles Unified School District (LAUSD) and stemmed from the work of an MLL task force made up of district administrators and content specialists. I was a literacy specialist working closely with a consultant to Local District 6 named Dr. Linda J. Carstens. Together, we, as well as a small group of interested members, designed professional-development experiences in order to bring coherence and alignment to the needs of MLLs within their district. Much of the early work of implementing and refining MLL shadowing then occurred in Hayward Unified School District, as well as Norwalk–La Mirada Unified School District in Norwalk, California, where all of the videos included in this book were filmed (see www.resources.corwin .com/MLLshadowing).

DEVELOPMENT OF THE SHADOWING PROCESS

The MLL shadowing protocol itself was built around the 2002 work of Pauline Gibbons's *Scaffolding Language, Scaffolding Learning*. After Local District 6 administrators had completed a book study around the Gibbons text, they decided that they wanted a culminating exercise that would allow them to apply their new learning about MLLs in context. The MLL shadowing protocol was designed specifically from Chapters 2 and 6 of the Gibbons book, which discusses academic speaking, as well as the listening demands of this student group. Both academic speaking and listening are underdeveloped domains that scaffold what are considered the literacy domains of reading and writing. If educators develop the academic speaking of MLLs, they are assisting with the development of student writing, as both speaking and writing are productive skills. As August and Shanahan (2006) suggest, speaking is the foundation of literacy for MLLs. James Britton also reminds us that, "Reading and writing sit on sea of talk." Similarly, both listening and reading are about input or receptive skills. When we require MLLs to actively listen, we are modeling and scaffolding active reading processes. For example, if students can actively listen and paraphrase what their partner has said, this is a similar process in reading to summarization. It is important to reinforce and provide professional development around these two domains of language before an educator ever enters a classroom to shadow an MLL (this is reinforced in Chapters 4 and 5 of this book) so that a participant understands what he or she is observing during the MLL shadowing experience. This process, in these stages, allows educators to have the same lens and alignment around what is being observed in a classroom setting.

MLL shadowing, then, is a technique for examining specific areas of an MLL's schooling experience and gaining insight into the student's perspective about school. The shadowing project involves selecting an MLL (the selection can be at random or at a predetermined English language proficiency level) and following the student for 2 to 3 hours, noting academic speaking and listening experiences at every 5-minute interval. The purpose of student shadowing is to gather information about the daily life of an ELL in order to participate in a larger conversation on improving the educational experiences of this group of students. The experience begins at the individual MLL student level, because as educators within educational systems, we look at groups of students and subgroups, but we often do not have the opportunity to observe the instructional experiences of individual students. Many times, we become overwhelmed by the specific linguistic and cultural needs of subgroups of students, and it is easier to turn away. The group results from the MLL shadowing experience can certainly be generalized and leveraged, as patterns and themes are analyzed, but it is first essential to explore what it is like to go through school needing to do "double the work"—that is, processing both language and content.

In a school or district context, teachers may engage in MLL shadowing projects in which they follow a student at a particular English language proficiency level for several hours (depending on the kind of MLL that is most common in that district). Educators are invited to gain an understanding regarding the student's academic speaking and listening needs as experienced through the process while obtaining qualitative data about the student's academic life through the specific comments documented.

TYPES OF SHADOWING PROJECTS

Since 2003, countless shadowing projects have been conducted across California and in New York, Illinois, and New Mexico. A large-scale shadowing project was conducted in New York through the New York Regional Bilingual Education Resource Network (RBERN), which assists schools and districts across all five boroughs in creating professional learning communities addressing English language learner issues. This project resulted in several follow-up presentations on creating environments for classroom and academic talk over several years, so that there was follow-up support for the teachers who participated in the shadowing project. Shadowing has also been used in the dual-language immersion (DLI) setting through a California Association for Bilingual Education (CABE) bilingual teacher and administrator pipeline program. DLI shadowing can assist schools or strands within schools in analyzing their language allocation plans and/or ensuring that MLLs are provided with equitable language and learning opportunities in DLI programs. In this way, shadowing projects can take on different foci. For example, in Rialto Unified School District in Southern California, the district, in its second year of implementing shadowing projects, decided to focus on MLL and students with special needs shadowing due to their overidentification of MLLs in special education. Both in Hayward Unified in Northern California and in Rialto Unified, shadowing projects were also conducted to bring attention to the needs of their standard English learners (SELs) while also bridging their academic language needs with those of MLLs. Lastly, MLL shadowing projects have also been conducted with preservice teachers at several universities in Southern California, including Whittier College, Biola University, and Claremont Graduate University. The MLL shadowing project is essential for preservice teachers so that they experience how to undo classroom silence before they ever step into the classroom setting. Preservice teachers then learn how to design lessons and units that assist them with disrupting silence in the classroom setting.

MLL Shadowing Processes

During Day 1 of the professional development session, participants are trained using a protocol in which they are taught how to monitor the domains of listening and academic speaking at the start of every 5-minute intervals for at least 2 consecutive hours. It is important to note that participants are not ready to formally shadow MLLs until they have studied both the elements of academic talk and the different forms of listening in the classroom, which they will later monitor in a classroom setting (see Chapters 4 and 5). In a professional development setting, participants do not shadow an MLL until the morning of Day 2 after they have amply studied academic speaking and listening on Day 1 of the training. Figure 2.1 is a sample MLL shadowing schedule.

This process of preparation for MLL shadowing on Day 1 of professional development ensures reliability of data collection while making sure that everyone is on the same page regarding what they are observing in the classroom setting. In the end, the research that is presented and strategies (Think-Pair-Share, Frayer model, and reciprocal teaching) that are modeled when participants are trained to shadow become the very techniques needed in the classroom in order to work toward systemically changing the absence of academic speaking and structured listening in classrooms. Chapter 3 describes my first MLL shadowing experience, including the analysis of student achievement data, the classroom observation, and the debriefing of the experience.

FIGURE 2.1 Sample Multilingual Language (MLL) Shadowing Schedule

MLL SHADOWING SCHEDULE	
DAY 1: PREPARATION FOR SHADOWING	**DAY 2: SHADOWING DEBRIEF AND THINK-PAIR-SHARE 2.0 DEBRIEF/INTRODUCTION TO FRAYER MODEL**

• AM—Speaking and Listening Session
 	
  o Data Introduction/Road to Reclassification
 	
  o How to Use the MLL Shadowing Protocol
 	
  o Detail regarding school assignments and MLL students
	• AM—Debriefing the MLL Shadowing Experience and Next Steps for Systems
	
	• Debriefing implementation of Think-Pair-Share 2.0 with Tuning Protocol

• PM—Introduction to Academic Language Development Strategy #1: Think-Pair-Share 2.0 • Homework: Shadow between Days 1 and 2 of professional development (this may be the following day or another day due to subs); implement Think-Pair-Share 2.0 in your classroom and bring back student work samples	• PM—Introduction to Academic Language Development Strategy #2: Frayer Model • Homework: Implement Frayer model strategy in your classroom and bring back student work samples

ROAD TO RECLASSIFICATION AND SHADOWING CONNECTIONS

Day 1 of MLL shadowing typically begins with an emphasis on a process called the Road to Reclassification, which is a project that was developed when first working on MLL shadowing with Los Alisos Middle School in Norwalk, California. Reclassification out of English learner status (California and federal label) and into mainstream courses is the first step that MLLs must take in order to receive access to more rigorous coursework and additional academic expectations. In California, the most common reclassification criteria are as follows:

- **English Language Proficiency Assessments for California (ELPAC):** Overall English proficiency level of 4;

- **California Assessment of Student Performance and Progress (CASPP):** Demonstration of "basic skills" in English from an objective assessment that is also given to English-proficient students of the same age;

- Teacher evaluation (**grades and/or unit assessments**); and

- Parent notification

In California, MLLs have to meet all of the requirements above in 1 year in order to move out of MLL status. This is important so that MLLs can begin to take college preparatory courses and/or not have their electives taken away in order to take an English language development course in middle and high school. A study conducted in the Los Angeles Unified School District (LAUSD) by the Tomas Rivera Policy Institute (2009) suggested that MLLs who do not reclassify by the end of their middle school experience are twice as likely to drop out of high school. In all of these ways, reclassification is a high-stakes endeavor.

The Road to Reclassification process is a way to ensure that everyone within a system—teachers, students, and parents—knows the reclassification criteria and process in order to assist MLLs with meeting that goal. The process begins by making sure that everyone understands the criteria and that teachers lead students through the process of goal setting in order to meet the reclassification criteria. MLLs are given their current and past grades, as well as academic achievement scores, including ELPAC and CAASP, and are asked to analyze their strengths and areas of improvement. It is important to begin with strengths in order to build on the assets that MLLs bring to school. This is especially important as we combat deficit views and lowered expectations of MLLs, but also because we all want to be viewed from an assets base first. MLLs then reflect upon what they are learning about themselves as a learner and how they are taking advantage of different resources on campus. Lastly and most powerfully, MLLs then set trimester goals by answering the following questions:

- What is one area you want to work on?

- What steps can you take to help you succeed in that area?

- What is one thing that your parent can do to support you?

- What is one thing that your teacher can do to support you?

This process typically takes place during the MLLs' English language development time or class. It is essential that MLLs complete this process several times per year and is most commonly done when new grades are distributed. The notion of goal setting is a lifelong skill that MLLs can take away with them into other areas of their lives. It is also a way in which everyone within a system can take responsibility for MLL success. Figure 2.2 is the Road to Reclassification graphic organizer used with students in the Norwalk–La Mirada Unified School District.

FIGURE 2.2   Road to Reclassification Academic Goal Setting Organizer

Road to Reclassification: Academic Goal Setting

My Name is: _____

My Grade is: _____ My ID number: _____

Years in the United States: _____ ELD Teacher: _____

CURRENT GRADES	1ST SEMESTER (LAST SCHOOL YR)	2ND SEMESTER (LAST SCHOOL YR)
Math: _____	Math: _____	Math: _____
Science: _____	Science: _____	Science: _____
History: _____	History: _____	History: _____
English: _____	English: _____	English: _____
Elective/PE: _____	Elective/PE: _____	Elective/PE: _____
Elective: _____	Elective: _____	Elective: _____

CURRENT GRADES	3RD SEMESTER (LAST SCHOOL YR)	4TH SEMESTER (LAST SCHOOL YR)
Math: _____	Math: _____	Math: _____
Science: _____	Science: _____	Science: _____
History: _____	History: _____	History: _____
English: _____	English: _____	English: _____
Elective/PE: _____	Elective/PE: _____	Elective/PE: _____
Elective: _____	Elective: _____	Elective: _____

My greatest strength is: _____

My area of need is: _____

What am I learning about myself as a multilingual learner?

What resources are you taking advantage of?

- ☐ Attending after-school tutoring/homework help
- ☐ Monitoring grades on Ayres (data system)
- ☐ Communicating with teacher(s)
- ☐ Setting a homework routine
- ☐ Using an agenda

Goal Setting

First Semester:

What is the one area you want to work on? _____

_____

What steps can you take to help you succeed in that area?

- _____

- _____

- _____

What is one thing that your parent can do to support you?

- _____

What is one thing that your teacher can do to support you?

- _____

Districts oftentimes find the Road to Reclassification process to be complementary to the MLL shadowing project, as both will assist with bringing awareness and creating systems of support for MLLs. Both projects should also be ongoing: The Road to Reclassification should continue for MLLs when they receive new grades and until they reclassify, while MLL shadowing projects can be used at first for baseline data collection and then for progress-monitoring purposes.

REFERENCES

August, D., & Shanahan, T. (2006). *Developing literacy in second-language learners: Report of the National Literacy Panel on Language Minority Children and Youth.* Mahwah, NJ: Lawrence Erlbaum Associates.

Gibbons, P. (2002). *Scaffolding language, scaffolding learning: Teaching second language learners in the mainstream classroom.* Portsmouth, NH: Heinemann.

Norwalk–La Mirada Unified School District. (2012). *Road to reclassification goal setting process.* Norwalk, CA: Author.

Tomas Rivera Policy Institute. (2009). *¿Qué pasa? Are English language learning students remaining in English learning classes too long?* Los Angeles, CA: Author.

CHAPTER 3

A Day in the Life of Josue, a Multilingual Learner

According to Fix, McHugh, Terrazas, and Laglagaron (2008), a 2006 report by the National Migration Institute indicated that a large percentage of multilingual learners (MLLs)—64%—were born in the United States. Josue, the first student I ever shadowed, was no different. He was in the 11th grade, and by the time our paths crossed at one of the largest high schools in California, with a total population of 5,600 students, he had been in U.S. schools for 11 years. I met Josue first on paper, as I had been given his most recent school picture so that I could identify him when I got into his first-period classroom. In the picture provided, Josue wore a sweatshirt with a hood and a white T-shirt underneath—what seemed to be typical teenage attire. He had the beginnings of a mustache, which traced over a bit of a smile along his lips. His eyes seemed kind as they peered out at me from the photo, something that I would confirm when I first saw Josue in person in the classroom setting. His eyes, however, seemed to want to say more than he was able to say. This was perhaps the voicelessness and invisibility that he had learned to get by with in the classroom setting. In his school picture, Josue appeared to somehow be making himself smaller as he hunched over a bit—it was as if he were there but not really fully there.

STUDENT PROFILE OF JOSUE

When I found Josue, his eyes gazed beyond the walls of his classroom and teacher to activities (perhaps soccer, as I heard him talk to his friend about a pick-up game). For most of the class session, Josue was slumped over, staring at his textbook, perhaps hoping that the answers and learning would become clearer for him if he only looked longer or harder. As I analyzed his grades from the profile form provided by the school, I looked for strengths and noticed that Josue was progressing well in English Language Development (ELD) and Algebra II. Teacher comments suggested that Josue was particularly talented in mathematics, where he came alive in the classroom setting and was able to demonstrate his academic identity. He also really enjoyed his ELD class, as this was where he experienced the most community with his peers and rapport with his teacher.

He struggled most with the subject areas that I would shadow him in—English and biology. At the time, Josue was in an English course in which he had received a C and a 2-year biology course in which he had earned a D. Both courses were labeled as "sheltered," meaning that content should be taught alongside language. In the classrooms in which I shadowed Josue, there was little content or language going on, as the students were virtually teaching themselves. Instead of receiving scaffolded instruction and the direct support that he needed, Josue sat through mindless exercises and silent worksheets. Both seemed to suck the joy out of learning for him, but still he persevered. This seemed to be a very different student than his math and ELD courses suggested. According to his attendance records, he had only missed 1 day of school that year and his teachers stated that he "behaved well."

ACHIEVEMENT RESULTS

Josue's cumulative grade point average (GPA) was 2.9091 (out of 4.0), which was almost a B average, even though he had only earned 60 credits toward graduation by the 11th grade (most schools in California require between 220 and 230 credits). If Josue wanted to graduate on time, he had some serious catching up to do. He needed additional mentoring and support to get him there, perhaps by his math or ELD teachers. Some of the courses that he was taking weren't even *a–g* courses, a sequence of high school courses that students in California must complete with a C or better to be *minimally* eligible for admission to the University of California (UC) or the California State University (CSU) system. These courses represent the basic level of academic preparation that high school students should achieve to undertake university work. It seemed that before I even entered the classroom, the odds were stacked against Josue. I thought to myself that there had to be a way to leverage the success that Josue had experienced in math and ELD into his other subject areas.

On the English Learner Proficiency Assessments for California (ELPAC), which is an English language proficiency assessment, Josue was making steady progress. His Reading and Writing scores were Moderately Developed (Level 3), but his Listening was Somewhat Developed (Level 2) and his Speaking was Minimally Developed (Level 1). Unfortunately, many MLLs have not been informed of the importance of the ELPAC. Many MLLs have seen this assessment once a year since they first entered school but do not take it seriously, especially because many educators also do not realize its importance. In fact, the ELPAC is the first hurdle that MLLs must clear before they truly begin to encounter rigorous, grade-level curricula. A study by the Tomas Rivera Policy Institute (2009) suggests that MLLs in the Los Angeles Unified School District (LAUSD) who demonstrated proficiency in English on the ELPAC by as late as the eighth grade had significantly improved academic outcomes.

Josue's poor academic scores seemed to be a foreshadowing of what I would see when I observed him in the classroom. Josue was not required to say one word, and neither were most of the students in his class. He also did not receive any direct instruction on the content introduced. Instead, he silently read his textbook and tried to make sense of the material before him. He was, in essence, teaching himself that day, and I wondered how many days like this Josue had had throughout his schooling experience. Perhaps that was why he was not progressing academically as he should have. I had a feeling that the lack of instruction and care around his instructional progress were more the norm as I reviewed the rest of his assessment progress and spent the day in two of his classrooms.

MINI DATA TALK

Josue's grade-level assessment result on the California Assessment of Student Performance and Progress (CAASPP) was Level 3 (Standard Met) for mathematics and Level 2 (Standard Not Met) for English. CAASPP results in English language arts/literacy (ELA) and mathematics give one measure of how well students are mastering California's challenging academic standards. The skills called for by these standards—the ability to write clearly, think critically, and solve problems—are essential for preparing students for college and a 21st-century career. Again, Josue's academic strength seemed to be in mathematics, which could be leveraged in other classes.

Josue had also not yet passed the California High School Exit Exam (CAHSEE), which measures the minimum skills and requirements for graduation in California and which is set at the ninth-grade level. Additionally, out of a class of 519, Josue, even with what seemed to be the least bit of instruction, was right near the middle of his class, standing at 271. With these kinds of scores, it seemed that the instructional damage that had been done to Josue was also going on for others.

PERIOD 1: ALGEBRA II

I first "met" Josue in his first period Algebra II class on a gloomy day in May. The teacher provided a mini lesson in which she modeled key concepts regarding linear equations with several stopping points for partner talks. Josue eagerly took notes and actively listened by taking notes as the teacher provided modeling. He spoke to his partner using a sentence frame when they were asked open-ended questions by the teacher. The teacher then placed students into groups of four to collaboratively solve a linear equation. Each student had a different role as they solved linear equations, as the teacher was using reciprocal teaching to guide students in working together. One student was the summarizer, one was the questioner, one was the predictor, and one was the connector. Josue was the predictor this time, and he completed his role on a graphic organizer and then discussed the linear equation from that lens. For example, since Josue was the predictor, he predicted how he would solve the linear equation. The rest of his group members then used their roles as follows: The summarizer summarized the linear equation steps that the group would take to solve the equation, the questioner listed questions that they had about the equation, and the connector made connections between linear equations and another math concept. After students completed their individual roles, each student shared their thoughts, and they solved the linear equation together. Once students solved the linear equation in small groups, they selected a representative to share their findings with the whole class. Josue took the lead and shared his group's findings with the entire class. He used the same sentence frame that was practiced earlier in the day to share his group's findings. Josue clearly emerged as a leader in this class, was engaged, and seemed motivated by the content, teacher, and his classmates.

PERIOD 2: ENGLISH

Josue's second-period English class was the exact opposite. Here, he watched a video on *The Crucible*, which was a play that he had read in class. The visual depictions in the video clearly connected to the content that had been taught, but the vocabulary and lack of structured listening over an entire period proved to be difficult for Josue as well as for the rest of the class. Josue watched the video respectfully, perhaps making sense of some of the content. I watched Josue nod off a bit during the video, while several other students began to discuss unrelated topics toward the end of the period, but the teacher seemed satisfied that his teaching had been done for the day. With a little assistance, this lesson could have been helpful to Josue and his classmates. I could not help thinking that perhaps a listening guide could have been included with specific content or key vocabulary that Josue needed to actively listen for. The teacher could have started the class with a warm-up or "sponge" activity, encouraging students to discuss key points from the section of the play that they had just gone over. Students could have also stopped and pair-shared around key concepts during specific times in the video. Finally, Josue could have been required to reflect on his learning by completing an exit slip at the end of class, on which he would have written down key ideas he had learned from the video and questions he still had. All of these techniques would provide scaffolds for Josue and the rest of the class and accountability for the learning that took place via the video.

Debriefing the MLL Shadowing Experience

I left Josue's second-period classroom knowing full well that he had not spent 1 minute in academic language production that period. I was frustrated and knew that something had to be done for Josue to graduate from high school, as even though his first-period experience was positive, he was not faring well in other subject areas, except for ELD. Sadly, I also knew that there were many more students like Josue in this particular school system, as well as across California and the country as a whole. In this way, the problem was systemic. Days like this were the very example of opportunity gaps. Unfortunately, we do not systemically and coherently train teachers to meet the specific needs of Josue and thousands of students like him. As the literature suggests, we do not currently provide teachers with enough training to become effective with our neediest groups of students. How do we expect to get different results when we know that teachers need coherent and aligned professional development in order to improve their own skills and student learning?

One way of aligning systems and creating urgency around the needs of this group of students comes through the MLL shadowing project previously described with Josue. Leaders of systems and those who work within them do not often have the time to take a look at the needs and instructional experiences of one student. MLL shadowing forces us to look at the specific needs of one student and reflect on how the things we do and don't do every day, either positively or negatively, impact that student's instructional progress. It reminds us that Josue does not have time to waste working independently on a worksheet unless the activity has been carefully designed for him. It forces us to realize that Josue must have ample opportunities to produce academic speaking all day long in order to receive access to content. Once they have shadowed an MLL, several educators have said things like, "Once I got back into the classroom [after shadowing], I immediately changed around my instruction to create more classroom talk," and "The person talking the most is learning the most, and I'm doing the most talking!" (Soto, personal communication, 2003, 2006).

It is important to remember, however, that MLL shadowing is not a silver bullet; it is not a panacea. It alone will not revolutionize your school or district—MLL shadowing is only the beginning of the conversation and exploration around the needs of MLLs, but it *can* be a catalyst to propel the work forward. MLL shadowing creates the urgency that must be in place to bring about true change. It provides the self-reflection that teachers and systems do not often have the luxury of doing. MLL shadowing must be followed up with focused, coherent, and sustained professional development over time. This follow-up professional development should then be focused on what was not seen surrounding specific MLL needs in the classroom setting. For example, since Josue needed more academic speaking to be embedded in his English class, professional development should be targeted there. Josue needed to be *required* to speak and actively listen in all classes—only in these ways would he make meaning around the content. If we keep Josue's school experience in mind, both MLL shadowing and follow-up professional development can assist systems in changing practice. Educators no longer need to be convinced of the needs; they have now seen them before their very eyes, and it becomes difficult to turn away or teach in the same old way again.

REFERENCES

Fix, M., McHugh, M., Terrazas, A., & Laglagaron, L. (2008). *Los Angeles on the leading edge: Immigrant integration indicators and their policy implications.* Washington, DC: Migration Policy Institute.

Tomas Rivera Policy Institute. (2009). *¿Qué pasa? Are English language learning students remaining in English learning classes too long?* Los Angeles, CA: Author.

SECTION II
Research Base

CHAPTER 4

The Role of Academic Speaking

As MLL advocates, part of our role in education is to disrupt silence. We must assist and ensure that MLLs have full access to school and the curriculum by requiring academic speaking often in the classroom setting so that MLLs develop an academic identity and so that we foster democratic classrooms. As such, the role of academic speaking or academic discourse has become increasingly important for MLLs in the research literature. The National Literacy Panel (August & Shanahan, 2006), Goldenberg (2006), and Zwiers (2016) have also shed light on the importance of academic speaking in literacy development with MLLs. Specifically, August and Shanahan report an important finding that the foundation of literacy for MLLs is academic speaking. That is, MLLs must be given ample opportunities to use extended stretches of language in order to become proficient academically in reading and writing in English. Goldenberg (2006) also suggests that "opportunities to extend oral English skills are critical for MLL students" (p. 35). Similarly, Zwiers (2016) suggests the following elements are essential to conversational discourse, which assists with eliciting longer stretches of academic speaking:

- Conversational discourse is the use of language for extended, back-and-forth, and purposeful communication among people—in other words, conversational discourse should not be one way. It should be organic and natural.

- A key feature of conversational discourse is that it is used to create and clarify knowledge, not just transmit it—a two-way exchange or conversation is essential to conversational discourse. MLLs should not just be listening to information but also participating in its creation and have opportunities to clarify when needed.

- Language is not one solid tool but a dynamic and evolving mix of resources and flexible tools used to communicate, build, and choose ideas at any given moment—multiple scaffolds and strategies should be utilized to elicit classroom talk. The specific scaffolds should connect with the purpose of the conversation.

One way to view academic discourse is by unpacking the following quote by James Britton, an influential British educator at the UCL Institute of Education whose theory of language and learning helped guide research in school writing while shaping the progressive teaching of language, writing, and literature in both England and the United States. Britton (1983) suggests that "Reading and writing float on a sea of talk." This metaphor allows us to remember and further unpack the importance of academic talk as connected to what we typically think of as the higher-order thinking domains of language: reading and writing. In other words, students, especially MLLs, need academic speaking as a scaffold for reading and writing. MLLs make personal meaning out of more rigorous content through academic speaking. As such, speaking is a scaffold for both reading and writing.

Reading and writing float on a sea of talk.

Kinsella (2007) recognizes that an essential element of academic language itself is the explicit teaching of the register of academic speaking itself, which includes teaching the distinctions between social—basic vocabulary, grammar, and form and function of language—and academic—content-area vocabulary and syntax in context to reading and writing—language. It is also important to note that there are several components to academic language development, according to Kinsella (2007), including vocabulary development, syntax, grammar, and register. This definition of academic language will be used and addressed throughout the book, but only academic speaking will be addressed in this chapter for the purposes of preparing educators for the MLL shadowing experience.

Unfortunately, historically, we have believed that quiet classrooms are good classrooms. We have thought that rows of students who compliantly listen while the teacher imparts knowledge into empty receptacles are best practice. Instead, what we must develop in a classroom setting is a culture of talking often about academic topics. We must find the language in the curriculum and elicit the voices in our classrooms. Even the best of instructional materials or programs may not emphasize the importance of academic speaking in a classroom setting. This infusion of language must be done by educators via specific techniques and structures that *require* classroom talk (see Chapter 10 for specific techniques). This means that administrators within systems must give teachers the time and support to reinfuse academic speaking into instructional materials. In this way, administrators and teachers alike should not expect or favor silence when they walk into classrooms. In order to create more academic speaking opportunities, teachers must also be given the time to work in teams, by department or by grade level, in order to develop meaningful academic speaking tasks. There must be a commitment to academic talk by everyone in the system in order for MLLs to be successful throughout their schooling experiences.

THE 15-MINUTE RULE

In my own work with educators, I like to recommend what I call the 15-minute rule. This means a commitment on the part of the teacher to not lecture or talk for more than 15 minutes at a time. I recommend the 15-minute rule because this is about the length of time that most students can actively listen. Please note that younger children may not be able to listen actively for 15 minutes, so this rule can be adjusted to match the age of a child. For example, in Kindergarten, this would make it the 5- to 6-minute rule. The 15-minute rule begins with the teacher talking for about 15 minutes using visual scaffolds and/or vocabulary support as necessary. The classroom talk is then gradually released to students for a few minutes each via a partner talk for about 2 to 4 minutes (each student speaks for about 1–2 minutes). Open-ended questions for partner talks, which are quicker conversations to make personal meaning or to check for understanding, should be designed carefully. The teacher then continues direct instruction for about 10 to 11 minutes and stops again for student partner talks for 2 to 4 minutes. The teacher will then engage in her third mini lecture for 10 to 11 minutes but this time will engage MLLs in a Think-Pair-Share, which is an opportunity for a longer segment of academic thinking, writing, talking, paraphrasing, and consensus for about 10 minutes (explained further in Chapter 10). Since students take about 10 minutes for the Think-Pair-Share in the final segment, the teacher can monitor partner interactions and preselect student responses that can be shared in the last few minutes of class or for that hour. This time can be used for reflection and/or summarizing what was learned. The figure below visually represents each step in the 15-Minute Rule process. In a virtual setting, instead of having two partner talks, the teacher might use

---

FIGURE 4.1 15-Minute Rule Guidelines

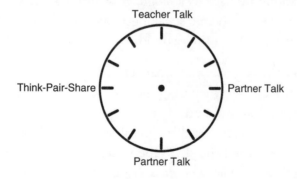

---

the chat box for engagement and ask a few students to unmute and respond further. The final Think-Pair-Share can happen in a breakout session.

TEACHER-GUIDED REPORTING

MLLs are often relegated to initiation-response-feedback (IRF) structures, whereby the students actually do very little talking (Gibbons, 2015). IRF is a process by which the teacher begins a conversation with a closed-ended question, such as "What color is the sky?" Such closed-ended questions require only a one- or two-word response and do not allow students to extend their discourse, vocabulary, or language sets. In this kind of exchange, the teacher usually ends such a conversation with "good job," and the conversation is considered over. Instead, Gibbons (2015), who has published widely on English language education, suggests an academic speaking structure called teacher-guided reporting (TGR), whereby the teacher and student together construct what the MLL cannot say on his or her own. This includes several oral language scaffolds in order to encourage MLLs to use and extend language, as follows.

FIGURE 4.2   Scaffolding Teacher-Guided Reporting

Strategies include

- Open-ended questions (multiple entryways/no one-word responses)
- Clarifying questions (linguistic, more detail, complete sentences)
- Encouragement (taking language risks)
- Recasting (restating in academic terms)

SOURCE: Adapted from Gibbons (2015).

- **Open-ended questions**—In contrast to closed-ended questions, which require only a one-word response, open-ended questions extend language, because there are multiple entryways and more than one way to formulate a response. An example of an open-ended question would be, "What do you notice about the sky?" (instead of "What color is the sky?," which only requires a one-word response). This question could be answered in a variety of ways and requires more descriptive and specific language, as well as longer stretches of language. When open-ended questions are used as a language scaffold, MLLs benefit greatly, as they get to extend their academic speaking repertoire. This strategy can also be used on its own or with the entire scaffolding technique of TGR.

- **Clarification**—After posing an open-ended question, teachers should ask for clarification of language, including more descriptive or specific language or a particular grammatical structure. For example, if a student answers that he notices that the sky is blue, the teacher can follow-up with "What shade of blue?" or "What do you like about the sky?" The teacher may also require the student to complete the response using a language stem, such as "I noticed that the sky is light blue with hints of white clouds." If students cannot produce such language on their own due to their current level of language proficiency, language stems such as "I noticed that the sky is _____ and _____" can be a helpful scaffold, so that students are focusing on content and not language. Such language stems should also grow and change as the school year progresses and as the MLL's language proficiency develops. More language stems have been included in the Academic Language Development Resources in Appendix B.

- **Encouragement**—When learning a second language, encouragement is helpful so that students are more likely to take language risks. When students panic or are not comfortable, they are more likely to shut down or not be willing to share responses publicly. Authentic encouraging responses such as "You're doing fine" and "Keep going" should be used with students often so that they are comfortable with taking language risks. Additionally, teachers should be sure to create a culture of language safety in the classroom setting by developing norms for classroom talk. That is, students should not be allowed to make fun of each other for errors or language inversions.

- **Recasting**—Students are also more likely to shut down and oftentimes do not want to practice language when they are overly corrected or put on the spot for a language mistake. Instead, recasting is a strategy by which a student's response is restated in academic terms. For example, if a student says, "That book is bery good," the teacher can recast, "So, you think the book is very good. Tell me why." This language correction does not put the student on the spot but also does not allow the error to go unnoticed or to be fossilized. The teacher can then follow-up with having the student repeat the sentence with the correct vocabulary embedded. Historically, when students have made language errors, teachers have either left such errors unaddressed or inappropriately and overly corrected students. This process of recasting ensures that errors are dealt with appropriately. MLLs are neither let "off the hook" nor are they shamed for language inversions.

GRAPHIC ORGANIZER FOR TEACHER-GUIDED REPORTING

The Graphic Organizer for TGR included in this chapter is a way for teachers to internalize and plan for all four steps in the TGR process. Notice that teachers are first encouraged to "think through" the objective of the lesson, which is often associated with the academic content standards being addressed but should also address the language standards and objectives. Teachers should then think about the content and language scenarios in which they would like to use TGR. For example, TGR should not be used "cold" in a classroom setting. Rather, MLLs should have some familiar and common academic experience, whereby they have developed some background knowledge, in order to have an academic conversation. Once teachers have internalized this process, they can then use all four steps—either together or independently—in a classroom setting to create more academic dialogue about recent topics. Figure 4.3 is the Teacher-Guided Reporting Organizer, which can be used for lesson-planning purposes.

FIGURE 4.3 Teacher-Guided Reporting Organizer

Content Objective: _____

_____

Language Objective: _____

_____

Open-Ended Question *(multiple entry points/no one-word responses)*	**Clarifying Questions** *(linguistic, more detail, complete sentences)*
Encouragement *(taking language risks)*	**Recasting** *(restating in academic language)*

SOURCE: Adapted from Gibbons (2015).

Benefits of Language Talk for MLLs

Not all classroom talk is effective talk or the kind of academic speaking that we want to occur in a classroom setting, but there are definite ways that MLLs benefit from language opportunities in a classroom setting. Specifically, according to Gibbons (2015) in *Scaffolding Language, Scaffolding Content*, MLLs benefit from language opportunities in the following ways:

- **Hear more language**—When MLLs talk to each other, they hear more language from a variety of sources. Instead of just hearing a message from the teacher, MLLs benefit from message redundancy and message abundancy—that is, hearing the message several times and in several different ways. The teacher should not be the only language model in the classroom setting. Students, especially when paired or grouped appropriately (high with low), can become language models for each other.

- **Practice more language**—MLLs oftentimes go home to communities where another language is spoken or where another variation of English is spoken—for example, Chicano English or Hawaiian Pidgin, which is an asset. Therefore, MLLs benefit from as many structured opportunities to talk to each other and the teacher as possible. Such language exchanges must be planned in advance in order for them to actually occur. Teachers must find those places in the curriculum for specific language moments.

- **More comfortable about speaking**—MLLs are more likely to take language risks with each other rather than in a whole-group setting. When students interact with each other in a structured format, they are more likely to take additional language turns. Structuring and modeling productive academic language, however, is the goal—so that students practice the appropriate kind of language needed and so that teachers do not become frustrated by inappropriate language usage. Figure 4.4 summarizes the benefits of productive group work for MLLs (see Chapter 2).

FIGURE 4.4 Summary of Productive Group Work for MLLs

1. *They hear more language.*	
2. *They speak more language.*	
3. *They understand more language.*	
4. *They ask more questions.*	
5. *They are more comfortable about speaking.*	

SOURCE: Adapted from Gibbons (2015).

Despite the many language benefits suggested by Gibbons (2015), teachers might still be wary of allowing talk in the classroom for fear of management issues or that the wrong kinds of conversations may ensue. It is important to note that classroom talk must be modeled and practiced before movement into independent practice. Specific ways to set up academic oral language development will be explored in Chapter 10.

MLLs also benefit from productive group work, but not all group work is effective or productive. Unfortunately, many educators recall poor experiences with group-work structures, in which they perhaps did most of the work for the group or not much work got done at all. These poor models were not effective and productive group work. For group work to be productive, it must be modeled and practiced as a whole class before students are expected to independently engage in group work themselves. According to Gibbons (2015), eight characteristics of productive group work must be taught explicitly for group work to be effective so that it can then elicit more academic talk in the classroom setting:

1. **Clear and explicit instructions are provided.** Students, especially MLLs, must know what is expected of them before they are expected to complete a task. From classroom noise levels to assignment details and time limits—all of these expectations must be made clear and modeled in order for students to be successful in the classroom. This means that teachers must have thought through each of these details before a group-work structure is utilized. For example, if a teacher is going to have a group of four for a group-work structure, how will she keep each student on task and accountable? How long will it take to complete the task? How will each student role be assessed? Will there be both group and individual accountability? More about each of these components will be explored in Chapter 10 after MLL shadowing has been completed.

2. **Talk is necessary for the task.** When educators place students in groups, they must *require* student talk. The kind of talk—academic in nature—must be carefully designed, but we should not put students into groups and then expect them to be silent. In fact, the assignments within those groups should organize the talking task so that it is both academic in nature and productive. Again, planning for necessary talk that is both structured and productive is essential to group-work tasks. Each student in the group should be held responsible for academic talk with a specific task and accountability for language. This can be done by providing language stems that can be used with each specific group role (examples of this can be found in Chapter 10).

3. **There is a clear outcome.** MLLs must know that they will be held accountable for group-work tasks. This means that each student should have a specific role that is appropriately tailored to the standards and objectives associated with the assignment. Additionally, the task should be

linguistically and cognitively appropriate so that student progress can be monitored. For example, if a student is a beginning-level English speaker, he or she should be provided with additional language and content scaffolds in order to be successful with the assignment. This might mean providing the student with both language stems for academic language practice (see Appendix B) as well as a word wall for vocabulary development within the content area. MLLs at higher levels of English language development may need more sophisticated language stems that demonstrate how to have academic conversations, as well as vocabulary word walls to be successful with academic vocabulary. Determining each MLL's specific language need is helpful with this process.

4. **The task is cognitively appropriate.** Group-work tasks should not be too simple or too difficult to be completed within a group setting. This notion fits well with Vygotsky's (1986) 1936 zone of proximal development (ZPD), or the gap between what a learner can do with or without additional assistance or scaffolding. A student should work in a group when a particular task is just too difficult to be completed on one's own. That is, there should be cognitive challenge associated with the talk. Additionally, group work can be assigned when the teacher determines that a particular skill or concept takes multiple repetitions to fully internalize. For MLLs to benefit from group work, the tasks should be talking oriented, causing students to make deeper meaning by using academic language to work through key concepts. The task should also lend itself to working together in order for there to be success with the task.

5. **The task is integrated with a broader topic.** Group-work tasks should integrate academic and linguistic objectives. That is, group-work structures that promote academic language should not be taught outside of the content. For example, after students read already required text selections, they can complete reciprocal teaching roles in order to keep them on task and accountable. This sort of exercise combines both group work and content. It also allows educators to amplify the academic speaking oftentimes taken out of the curriculum. When students talk about and not merely read texts, they will make deeper meaning around the content and also practice language. Procedures for how to set up reciprocal teaching are introduced in Chapter 10 as a way to systemically elicit more academic oral language development after MLL shadowing has been completed.

6. **All students are involved.** Each MLL should be held accountable for both academic speaking in groups and an individual academic task so that comprehension can be monitored. If each student in a group does not have a task or role, he or she is less likely to practice language and benefit from the group-work interaction due to lack of accountability. Additionally, each

student should be given multiple academic speaking stems so that he or she understands how to participate in academic discourse.

7. **Students have enough time.** MLLs should be given enough time to complete tasks. If students are given too much time, they are off task. If they have too little time, they are more likely to get frustrated. When teachers plan for a particular assignment or activity, they should estimate the amount of time students need to complete tasks. Teachers can then use timers to monitor student activity as well as to ensure that they are not losing precious instructional time. I typically start students off with an initial amount of time—somewhere between 10 and 20 minutes, depending on the task—and then adjust the time depending on how students are progressing. It is essential that the teacher monitor group work by walking around the room (what I call the power walk) in order to determine how much additional time students may need to be successful with a task or assignment.

8. **Students know how to work in groups.** It is important for educators to utilize the gradual release of responsibility to an independent practice model in order for students to be successful with group work. That is, teachers should never expect students to be able to complete a task on their own without ample modeling. One way to do this is to use the fishbowl approach, whereby a pair or group of students comes to the front of the classroom, and they model what effective partner talks or group conversations look like. The teacher should work with students who will model ahead of time in order to ensure that appropriate modeling is provided. Providing this level of scaffolding will allow students to be successful with group work. Teachers will also be less frustrated with issues when they arise. Although modeling takes time at the beginning, it ensures that fewer problems occur in the end for both the teacher and the student. Figure 4.5 is a summary of the characteristics of effective group work described previously.

FIGURE 4.5 Characteristics of Effective Group Work for MLLs

1. Clear and explicit instructions are provided.
2. Talk is necessary for the task.
3. There is a clear outcome.
4. The task is cognitively appropriate.
5. The task is integrated with a broader topic.
6. All children are involved.
7. Students have enough time.
8. Students know how to work in groups.

SOURCE: Adapted from Gibbons (2015).

Monitoring Academic Speaking During MLL Shadowing

According to August (2003), since MLLs spend less than 2% of their school day in academic speaking, it is an eye-opening and self-reflective experience for educators to monitor academic speaking specifically over the course of 2 hours of MLL shadowing. What Soto has found in shadowing projects across the country is that post Common Core, MLLs appear to be spending between 5–10% of their school day in academic speaking. Gibbons (2015) suggests that it should be around 30%. Only after educators have understood the literature and the importance of academic speaking in a classroom setting are they ready to monitor academic speaking in a classroom setting. Once educators have been provided with a profile of the MLL, they will shadow for 2 hours (this will be provided by training organizers; see Chapter 6) and begin tracking his or her academic speaking at every 5-minute interval (at least 2 hours is the recommended time when shadowing).

It is important that participants understand that they are monitoring what they see first at the start of the 5-minute interval and not for the entire 5-minute interval itself. For example, if an MLL begins the start of the 5-minute interval by writing, but in that same 5-minute interval turns and talks to a partner, only the writing activity should be coded. Whatever happens after the start of the 5-minute interval will be included under comments. This is important for interrater reliability reasons—that is, so that everyone is using the same structure and procedure when monitoring their MLL. Additionally, it is important to note that the purpose of shadowing is to explore a day in the life of an MLL. The process is not a running record but a way to gather general trends and patterns in academic speaking and active listening for MLLs within a school system. Similarly, in order to ensure interrater reliability, educators should also use the codes shown in Figure 4.6 for every 5-minute interval being monitored.

FIGURE 4.6   MLL Shadowing Codes

Primary Speaker	Mostly to Whom?	Primary Speaker	Mostly to Whom?	
Your Student	1. Student	**Teacher**	5. Student	**SPEAKING**
	2. Teacher		6. Small Group	
	3. Small Group		7. Whole Class	
	4. Whole Class			

MLL Shadowing Codes for Academic Speaking

The codes will be checked off on the MLL Shadowing Protocol Form (see Figure 4.5 for speaking). The purpose is to monitor, at the start of every 5-minute interval, what the primary speaker—either the MLL or teacher—is doing in terms of academic speaking. Again, it is important to remember that whatever is occurring at the *start* of the 5-minute interval is what should be monitored. The MLL shadowing form is not a running record, whereby everything within that time period is written down. Instead, educators should only take down what is happening *most* at the beginning of that 5-minute time frame so that general trends and patterns can be discussed within a system. Figure 4.5 is a blank of the academic speaking section of the MLL Shadowing Protocol Form (for the full form, see Figure 7.3 on page 74; Appendix A, page 136; or http://www.corwin.com/MLLshadowing).

Although the purpose of MLL shadowing is to monitor the MLL's academic speaking and listening, there will be times when the student is not the primary speaker because the teacher is talking. Therefore, there are two sets of codes, one for students and one for the teacher. When the student is speaking, Codes 1 through 4 should be checked off. When the teacher is talking, Codes 5 through 7 should be checked off. For example, if the MLL student is speaking to a partner, then Box 1 should be checked off, as noted in Figure 4.6. The process of coding specific academic speaking modes over a 2-hour period allows educators to see firsthand the lack of academic oral language development opportunities experienced by MLLs in a classroom setting. When groups of educators complete this project, we begin to see how this relative silence begins to negatively impact instruction for MLLs.

FIGURE 4.7 Blank Academic Speaking Section

ACADEMIC SPEAKING (CHECK ONE)	COMMENTS
☐ Student to Student—1 ☐ Student to Teacher—2 ☐ Student to Small Group—3 ☐ Student to Whole Class—4 ☐ Teacher to Student—5 ☐ Teacher to Small Group—6 ☐ Teacher to Whole Class—7	

FIGURE 4.8 Academic Speaking Coded for MLL

ACADEMIC SPEAKING (CHECK ONE)	COMMENTS
☑ Student to Student—1 ☐ Student to Teacher—2 ☐ Student to Small Group—3 ☐ Student to Whole Class—4 ☐ Teacher to Student—5 ☐ Teacher to Small Group—6 ☐ Teacher to Whole Class—7	*Josue spoke to his elbow partner using a language stem.*

However, if the teacher is speaking to the whole class, then Box 7 should be checked off, as noted in Figure 4.9.

FIGURE 4.9   Academic Speaking Coded for Teacher

ACADEMIC SPEAKING (CHECK ONE)	COMMENTS
☐ Student to Student—1 ☐ Student to Teacher—2 ☐ Student to Small Group—3 ☐ Student to Whole Class—4 ☐ Teacher to Student—5 ☐ Teacher to Small Group—6 ☑ Teacher to Whole Class—7	*The teacher lectured to the whole class about climate change.*

COMMENTS SECTION OF MLL SHADOWING PROTOCOL FORM

In addition to the coding section of the shadowing observation form, there is also the comments section on the right-hand side of the form. This is a place where qualitative information, which cannot be captured merely by checking off a box, should be recorded. For example, if the teacher is talking but the student is struggling or not fully listening, this is the place where that information can be taken down. If the student is confused or something unusual is noticed, it can be written here. Additionally, this section is the place to write whatever happens beyond the top of the first 5-minute interval. That is, if at the start of the interval, the MLL is on task and working on his or her assignment but within the same 5-minute interval is off task, then the on-task behavior should be coded or checked off, but the off-task behavior will then be documented in the comments section. Anecdotal comments can also be noted here, as well as comments that are about the teacher and not the student.

Figure 4.10 is an example of the kind of comments that you might record when shadowing your MLL student.

FIGURE 4.10   Comments Section of MLL Shadowing Protocol Form

COMMENTS
Josue started this 5-minute interval by being on task with his quick write. He seemed to be really engaged and interested in the topic at first. Unfortunately, he quickly got off task and started talking off-topic to the person next to him. He seemed to struggle a bit with writing anything more than a couple of sentences.

The comments section of the MLL shadow observation form provides useful information during the debriefing session, so it is important to take down careful and copious notes that will allow patterns and themes from the observation to emerge. In the debriefing portion of the MLL shadowing training, educators will be asked to summarize their comments into a few sentences on a sticky note. From there, themes and patterns from all of the comments will assist with triangulating the classroom data that were coded for the academic speaking portion of the MLL Shadowing Protocol Form (this is described further in Chapter 7).

References

August, D. (2003). *Literacy and second-language learners*. Presentation to LAUSD: District 6 Administrators. Huntington Park, CA: LAUSD District 6 Offices.

August, D., & Shanahan, T. (2006). *Developing literacy in second-language learners: Report of the National Literacy Panel on Language Minority Children and Youth*. Mahwah, NJ: Erlbaum.

Britton, J. (1970). *Language and learning*. Coral Gables, FL: University of Miami Press.

Britton, J. (1983). Writing and the story of the world. In B. M. Kroll & C. G. Wells (Eds.), *Explorations in the development of writing: Theory, research, and practice* (pp. 3–30). New York: Wiley.

Gibbons, P. (2015). *Scaffolding language, scaffolding learning: Teaching second language learners in the mainstream classroom*. Portsmouth, NH: Heinemann.

Goldenberg, C. (2006, July 26). Improving achievement for English learners: What the research tells us. *Education Week*, pp. 34–36.

Kinsella, K. (2007). *Bolstering academic language and reading comprehension*. PowerPoint presentation at the Academic Language Development Workshop, Mountain View School, El Monte, CA. Available at http://www.sccoe.k12.ca.us/depts/MLL/kinsMLLa_2009.asp

Vygotsky, L. S. (1986). *Thought and language* (rev. ed.). Cambridge, MA: MIT Press.

Zwiers, J. (2016). *Academic language mastery: Conversational discourse in context*. Thousand Oaks, CA: Corwin.

CHAPTER 5

The Importance of Active Listening

Listening, like speaking, is an underdeveloped domain in most classrooms. Historically, we have overly emphasized reading and writing as the heavy-hitting domains that will be tested, making them somehow academically more important. Instead, we need to understand the interconnected nature of the domains of language: speaking as a scaffold for writing (a mental outline for the writing process) and listening as a scaffold for reading (both about comprehension and not merely discrete skills). Education reform leader Deborah Meier (2010) reminds us that "Teaching is listening, and learning is talking." At first glance, this quote seems counterintuitive. We have historically thought that teachers should do all of the talking and students should do the listening. However, as we learned in the last chapter, students make personal meaning through academic talk. As such, with listening, the role of the teacher should shift. It is not that teachers shouldn't talk at all in the classroom setting but instead that they should be intentional about their talking time and share it with their students. The role of the teacher, instead, needs to become more about listening to students and what their needs are and making sure to determine next instructional steps from what they've heard. For example, if, by listening to student conversations, the teacher hears an inversion, then reteaching might be needed. Or if the teacher hears that a student has a powerful idea from a conversation, the teacher might want to highlight that idea with the entire class. After all, if we want students to be active and effective listeners, then we need to model the process for them.

> "Teaching is listening, learning is talking."
>
> Deborah Meier

Part of the issue with listening is also that we often assume that students know how to listen, and we do not take the time to explicitly teach students how to do so—until, of course, students are off task and we become increasingly frustrated with them. In teacher education programs, unfortunately, preservice teachers are often not taught how to embed and plan for listening in their lesson planning or the classroom setting. For MLLs, however, learning *how* to actively listen, or the purpose of listening, and being required to do so becomes an important learning scaffold. Listening and reading are both about receptive skills, or making meaning from sounds or text. Spending time teaching your students, especially your MLLs, to listen is not in vain. It is a lifelong skill that will assist them. Additionally, when we assist students with the ways in which they can listen, we provide support and reinforcement for the ways in which they can read—either specifically or generally.

NUNAN'S QUADRANTS OF LISTENING

Nunan (1990) suggests that there are two contexts for listening—academic and social—with academic listening being the more difficult of the two, therefore requiring the most scaffolding or support. He also suggests that we can listen in two ways: (1) one-way listening, whereby we take in information without being able to clarify or ask questions, as in a lecture; and (2) two-way listening, whereby there is a dialogue of some sort, and students can be supported with questions and clarification. Figure 5.1 is a visual of Nunan's Quadrants of Listening, with examples of what happens in each kind of context (interpersonal/social vs. information based/academic).

FIGURE 5.1 Nunan's Quadrants of Listening With Modified Example

Two-Way Listening (Dialogue)			
Interpersonal (social) topics	**Quadrant A** *Taking part in* • Conversation at a party • Conversation at a bus stop about the weather • A chatty phone call to a friend	**Quadrant C** *Taking part in* • A job interview • A conversation involving giving directions or instructions • A phone inquiry about buying a computer	**Information based (academic)**
	Quadrant B *Listening to* • Someone recounting a personal anecdote • Someone telling a story • Someone telling a joke	**Quadrant D** *Listening to* • The radio or TV news • A lecture • Phone information (e.g., instructions for paying a bill)	
One-Way Listening (Lecture)			

SOURCE: Adapted from Nunan, D. (1990).

When shadowing an MLL, educators are asked to monitor the kinds of listening that students are required to participate in within a classroom setting at every 5-minute interval, as per Nunan's Quadrants of Listening. Educators then check off the appropriate section for listening, much like it is described in the academic speaking chapter.

CODING FOR ACADEMIC LISTENING

Figure 5.2 is a blank listening form to be used during MLL shadowing. Notice that there are two sections to the academic listening portion of the protocol. On the left-hand side, there is a section for monitoring academic listening, either one way (lecture) or two way (dialogue or conversation). The section on the right asks educators to monitor whether the MLL is not required to listen or not listening at all.

FIGURE 5.2 Blank Listening Form

ACADEMIC LISTENING: ONE-WAY OR TWO-WAY (CHECK ONE)	STUDENT IS NOT LISTENING (CHECK ONE)
☐ Student listening mostly to student—1 ☐ Student listening mostly to teacher—2 ☐ Student listening mostly to small group—3 ☐ Student listening mostly to whole class—4 **Note: One-way (lecture) or two-way (dialogue)**	☐ Reading or writing silently—1 ☐ Student is off task—2

As they did with the academic speaking section of the MLL shadowing form, educators should code listening behaviors at the start of every 5-minute interval. Notice on the left-hand side of the MLL shadowing form that educators are only asked to monitor student listening. Unlike the academic speaking portion, there is no section to monitor teacher listening levels, so there are only four options to check off, as noted in the Academic Listening Codes section that follows. Notice also that there is an additional section for academic listening to be used when students are not listening. This can be coded in two different ways: (1) reading or writing silently, which does not require active listening; and (2) student is off task and should have been listening.

ACADEMIC LISTENING CODES

Figure 5.3 shows the MLL shadowing codes for academic listening, which are to be used when monitoring MLL listening behaviors only.

FIGURE 5.3 Shadowing Codes

LISTENING	
PRIMARY LISTENER	**LISTENING MOSTLY TO WHOM?**
Your Student	1. Student
	2. Teacher
	3 Small group
	4. Whole class

As demonstrated in the coding system, academic listening will be monitored as follows:

- A student listening mostly to another student, as during a Think-Pair-Share

- A student listening mostly to the teacher, as during a lecture or individual conference

- A student listening mostly to a small group, as in a group experiment or productive group work

- A student listening mostly to the whole class, as during a choral reading or singing

These four codes will allow educators to efficiently monitor the academic listening opportunities that MLLs are engaged in during a school day.

ACADEMIC LISTENING (ONE WAY OR TWO WAY)

In Figure 5.4, the listening portion of the MLL shadowing form has been coded as a 2 because the student was listening to the teacher during a science demonstration. At the start of the 5-minute interval, the teacher demonstrated the use of a beaker to transfer liquid from a bottle to a petri dish. The entire class, including the MLL, watched the teacher modeling this and the next steps for an experiment before students were separated into small groups to complete their own experiments.

FIGURE 5.4 Completed Form for Academic Listening

ACADEMIC LISTENING ONE-WAY OR TWO-WAY (CHECK ONE)
One-way (lecture) or two-way (dialogue)
☐ Student listening mostly to student—1
☑ Student listening mostly to teacher—2
☐ Student listening mostly to small group—3
☐ Student listening mostly to whole class—4

During the teacher modeling of the lab experiment described previously, the MLL actively listened and took notes on a graphic organizer provided by the teacher on how to replicate the experiment in the groups. Because the student was on task and actively taking notes, the second box of the academic listening section was checked off.

NOT LISTENING OR NOT REQUIRED TO LISTEN

The middle section of the MLL shadowing form requires educators to monitor when students are not listening or are not required to listen. Figure 5.5 is a blank MLL shadowing form to be used only when students are demonstrating one of these two behaviors.

FIGURE 5.5   Completed Form for Student Not Listening

STUDENT IS NOT LISTENING (CHECK ONE)

☐   Reading or writing silently—1

☐   Student is off task—2

When MLLs are not required to listen, as in reading or writing silently, their responses are coded in the far-right column as a 1. When students are off task and are supposed to be listening but are not, the response is coded as a 2. During the debriefing session, all of these codes will be added up so that themes and patterns can be determined for the group of MLLs shadowed at a particular school site.

Figure 5.6 is a shadowing form that has been coded a 1 because the MLL was completing an independent quickwrite assignment at the beginning of class. The student was on task and writing to the prompt, so the first box was checked off.

FIGURE 5.6   Completed Academic Listening Form

STUDENT IS NOT LISTENING (CHECK ONE)

☑   Reading or writing silently—1

☐   Student is off task—2

More description on how to use the MLL shadowing protocol and how to code listening and speaking specifically can be found in Chapter 7.

REFERENCES

Meier, D. (2010). Quote from Deborah Meier blog post. Available at https://deborahmeier.com

Nunan, D. (1990). Learning to listen in a second language. *Prospect*, *5*(2), 7–23. Available at http://www.ameprc.mq.edu.au/resources/prospect/V5_N2_1990

SECTION III

Preparation for Shadowing

CHAPTER 6

Preparing for a Shadowing Training

ORGANIZING AND SETTING UP A SHADOWING PROJECT

The following section describes what is needed to begin to organize a multilingual learner (MLL) shadowing training. It is important to note that the MLL shadowing training includes two parts, segmented into 2 days (either back to back or at least a month in between), as follows:

DAY 1: PREPARATION FOR TRAINING

AM: Background research on MLLs, academic language development, and training on listening and speaking

PM: Training on how to use the MLL shadowing protocol and directions for Day 2, and introduction to Think-Pair-Share

DAY 2: MLL SHADOWING AND DEBRIEFING

AM: MLL shadowing at school sites (this can also happen in between Days 1 and 2, if not back-to-back days)

PM: Debriefing the shadowing experience; debriefing implementation of Think-Pair-Share

In order for an MLL shadowing training to be successful, the organizers of the training must determine what English language development level, or kind of MLL, they would like their participants to shadow. For example, if many MLLs within a system are not making progress at the midway point in English language development, which is often common, then educators may choose to shadow MLLs at that level. If most MLLs within a system remain at the final levels of English language proficiency without becoming fluent in English, then participants should shadow there. Or if there are many newcomers in a particular system and there is a desire to target their needs, then shadowing commences here. In this way, each MLL shadowing training should be tailored to the specific needs of the particular students within that system. Typically, the MLL or categorical director will be responsible for creating MLL profiles, which include 3 years' worth of achievement data on each student being shadowed. It is helpful to have 3 years' worth of data so that educators can analyze trends and patterns in MLL achievement as well as really "get to know" the student before the shadowing experience.

DISTRICTWIDE MLL SHADOWING

When organizing a districtwide MLL shadowing training, it is important for district organizers to backward map the agenda, details, and information that will be needed. First, organizers will need to determine how many shadowing participants they will have in a particular training. The more participants that are included, the more MLL profiles will be needed for those participants to shadow on Day 2 of the training, which can also cause more of an impact at each school site. Once the numbers are determined, organizers will need to contact schools, often at the elementary, middle, and high school levels, to gain permission to shadow at those sites. For example, in Norwalk–La Mirada Unified School District in Norwalk, California, all administrators participated in MLL shadowing according to school level. Elementary school administrators shadowed MLLs on one day, middle school administrators on another day, and high school administrators on still another day. When each administrator had shadowed an MLL, everyone was called together for the debriefing session and for planning the next steps. Each of these days was a half-day session in order to reduce the amount of time that administrators were away from their school sites. Figure 6.1 is a sample agenda from the MLL shadowing trainings in the Norwalk–La Mirada Unified School District.

Similarly, in the Lucia Mar Unified School District in Arroyo Grande, California, 90 administrators, teachers, and district office staff members participated in a 2-day MLL shadowing experience, according to school level. After being trained on how to shadow on Day 1, each teacher and administrator was assigned to an MLL at an elementary, middle, or high school within the district and shadowed that student between Days 1 and 2 (these days were staggered in order to ensure

FIGURE 6.1 MLL Shadowing Agenda for Day 1

Norwalk–La Mirada Unified School District Day 1

MLL SHADOWING TRAINING

AGENDA

8:00—Welcome and Agenda Review

8:15—MLL Data/Academic Speaking Overview With Think-Pair-Share

10:00—Break

10:30—Listening Overview

- Shadowing Introduction/Practice With the Protocol Day 2 Agenda Overview/Logistics/ Student Profiles

12:00—Closing

PLEASE DON'T FORGET TO WEAR YOUR

DISTRICT ID TO THE OBSERVATION SCHOOL ON DAY 2.

that enough subs were available). Many individual schools within Lucia Mar Unified School District have also now shadowed MLLs at their own school sites so that more teachers could have the experience of shadowing.

As has been explained in previous chapters, MLL shadowing begins with training on the importance of academic speaking and listening for MLLs. This overview provides the grounding and ensures that everyone who is shadowing has the same lens by which to go into classrooms. Figure 6.2 is the agenda for Day 2 of the MLL shadowing training in the Norwalk–La Mirada Unified School District.

FIGURE 6.2 MLL Shadowing Agenda for Day 2

Norwalk–La Mirada Unified School District Day 2

MLL SHADOWING TRAINING AGENDA

School Site Visit Information

Johnston Elementary School (October 8th)

Meeting Room: G-2

Premeeting Time: 7:45 AM

Los Alisos Middle School (October 22nd)

Meeting Room: 104

Premeeting Time: 7:30 AM

John Glenn High School (October 29th)

Meeting Room: Library

Premeeting Time: 7:50 AM

8:00–10:00 AM—MLL Shadowing

10:00 AM—Break/Recess

10:25 AM—Shadowing Debrief

11:15 AM—Wrap, Evaluations, PD Survey, Next Steps

Note that the agenda for Day 2 includes details such as the premeeting time and meeting location. The premeeting location is where participants will meet at the school site before the actual shadowing occurs in classrooms. This brief time period allows the organizers to review the expectations and directions for shadowing that day. Additionally, during this time period, the MLL student profile will be distributed (for the full form, see Figure 6.5 on page 59; Appendix A, page 143; or http://www.corwin.com/MLLshadowing). The MLL student profile includes the student's schedule, room number, and language development level, as well as achievement data (a sample student profile is included on page 58). Typically, a school site representative will be present to assist with room number distributions and a map of the school. Some additional reminders to participants during the premeeting are included in Figure 6.3.

FIGURE 6.3 Dos and Don'ts of Shadowing

DO	DON'T
✓ Do shadow at the school level of your assignment.	✗ Don't ask for a boutique assignment.
✓ Do help become familiar with forms.	✗ Don't ask student any formal questions.
✓ Do help maintain focus on the student.	✗ Don't share any evaluative statements about teacher or class.

SOURCE: Adapted from Gibbons (2015).

DOS AND DON'TS OF SHADOWING

It is important for participants to shadow at the same level at which they teach or are administrators. This is especially important the first time that MLL shadowing is done so participants can be more reflective about their own specific settings and practices. If classrooms or schools are not similar to what educators encounter every day, it may be more difficult to leverage change from the experience because the students or community are so different. In the afternoon of Day 1 of the MLL shadowing training, participants are taught how to use the MLL shadowing protocol, much as it is described in Chapters 4 and 5. Participants should be reminded at the end of Day 1 that they should bring the sample protocol with them on Day 2 of the training. Additionally, training organizers should make enough copies of the MLL shadowing protocol, which often means three back-to-back copies so that participants can shadow their MLLs for 2 full hours (see blank copy in Appendix A, page 136). Organizers should review how to fill out the form during the preplanning portion of the onsite training at the school. Participants should also be reminded that focus should be maintained on the *student* and not the teacher or other students.

Student shadowing is about a day in the life of an MLL and not placing blame on any part of the system. Participants should also be reminded that neither the student nor teacher should be aware of the MLL who is being shadowed so the data collection is not impacted. All teachers at a school site should be alerted that classroom observations of MLLs in general are occurring, but they should not be told the specific students who are being shadowed. Lastly, participants should be reminded not to sit too close to their MLLs so that students do not become aware that they are being shadowed.

Don'ts of Shadowing

Participants should also be reminded of what should not occur during a shadowing observation both on the afternoon of Day 1 of the MLL shadowing training and at the premeeting on Day 2 of the training. Both organizers and participants should not ask teachers to provide a special or boutique lesson. Instead, teachers should do what they typically do when observers are not in the room, as participants are shadowing the student and not the teacher. Organizers of the training should also tell teachers that participants will be in rooms to learn from MLLs, but they should not indicate which specific student will be observed. This will ensure that teachers will not act any differently than normal toward that student. In this same vein, specific evaluative statements about the class or student should not be shared with the teacher so as to reinforce that the observation was about the student and not the teacher or classroom (the change in teacher practices comes in the follow-up professional development). Finally, participants should not interact with the MLL or other students in class. Participants should try to be as unobtrusive as possible, including placing cell phones in vibrate mode. All of these suggestions will ensure that the MLL shadowing training is as successful as possible.

DETERMINING MLL SHADOWING NUMBERS

Since each shadowing participant will need an MLL to shadow, it is important to determine training numbers early on. The organizers (district office staff members or school site administrators) will need to ensure that they have enough MLLs at corresponding school sites for those participants to shadow. For example, if a particular school site or school district has thirty participants at the elementary, middle, and high school levels at a particular training, it would need to make sure that it has at least one elementary, one middle, and one high school that is willing to host the shadowing event. Participants should shadow at the level of their daily work. Participants can also shadow in pairs in order to alleviate the impact on classrooms, but it is not recommended to have more than two observers in a classroom at one time, as it can be overwhelming for the teacher. Also, there often is not enough classroom space to comfortably house more than two observers in a room.

SELECTING MLLS FOR SHADOWING

Before the MLL shadowing event, it is also important to have organizers determine the English language proficiency level of need within the school or district so that information can be communicated to the school or district office when selecting students. If most MLLs are not making progress at the midrange of language ability, then shadowing should be done at that level of proficiency. If the district office can access school site MLL data, it is best that they create the MLL Student Profile for each of the sites so that schools do not have one more task on their plates. Figure 6.4 is an MLL Student Profile for Shadowing Form (also included in Appendix A page 143 and at http://www.corwin.com/MLLshadowing) that can be helpful as a guide regarding the demographic information and type of achievement data that will be needed for shadowing.

FIGURE 6.4   MLL Student Profile for Shadowing Form

Student Information

- First name
- Date of Birth
- Date of Entry in US
- Date of Entry in District

Test Results (last 3 years, if possible):

- Language Proficiency Assessment
- State Achievement Scores for ELA & Math
- Grades
- GPA
- High School Exit Exam Scores (HS only)

If the district office has access to the data for the school via a database, then it only needs to ask schools to provide a picture of each student to be shadowed. The picture is important so that shadowing participants can easily identify students in a classroom when observing. The first name of the student is important so that the shadowing participant can connect with the MLL as a human being. For privacy reasons, the last name of the student is not necessary. The date of birth and grade level are important so that the educator can compare the chronological age to the current grade level and English language development level that the student is in. All of this demographic information should be collected before a shadowing training and when determining final training capacity numbers. Figure 6.5, also included in Appendix A (page 143) and at http://www.corwin.com/MLLshadowing, lists the demographic information needed for the MLL to be shadowed.

FIGURE 6.5   Blank MLL Student Profile for Shadowing

- **Picture of MLL for visual identification**
- **First name**
- **Date of birth**
- **Grade level**
- **Date of entry into United States**
- **Date of entry into district**

Classes or Periods to Be Shadowed

PERIOD/CLASS	COURSE TITLE	TEACHER	ROOM #

Test Results (last 3 years, if possible)

ELPAC* OVERALL	LISTENING AND SPEAKING	READING	WRITING

*English Language Proficiency Assessments for California

CAASPP* FOR ELA** AND MATH	GRADES	GPA	CAHSEE*** (HS ONLY)

*California Assessment of Student Performance and Progress

**English language arts

***California High School Exit Exam

The dates of entry into the United States and into the district allow the educator to later analyze the level of progress that the student has made in terms of his or her English language proficiency. The goal in California is that MLLs should progress one language proficiency level per year; other states have determined their own Annual Measurable Academic Objective (AMAO). The English language proficiency level or language assessment data (in California, this is the ELPAC, or the English Language Proficiency Assessments for California) are helpful for progress monitoring analysis and to make initial recommendations regarding student need. Figure 6.6 shows how the English language proficiency data should be collected for each MLL shadowed.

FIGURE 6.6   Language Development Results

Test Results (last 3 years, if possible)			
ENGLISH LANGUAGE PROFICIENCY OVERALL	LISTENING AND SPEAKING	READING	WRITING

The state standardized or grade-level assessment data are helpful when monitoring annual grade-level academic progress (in California, this is the CAASPP, or the California Assessment of Student Performance and Progress). An MLL's grades, grade point average (GPA), and additional assessment scores also provide eye-opening information, especially as this information can be triangulated with the observation once MLL shadowing is completed. The classroom periods, teachers, and room numbers are important so educators can find and follow (at the secondary level) their respective MLL from classroom to classroom when shadowing. Figure 6.7 includes the sections to be completed for the state achievement results, grades, GPA, and high school exit exam results.

FIGURE 6.7   State Assessment Results and Class Schedule

Classes or Periods to Be Shadowed			
PERIOD/CLASS	COURSE TITLE	TEACHER	ROOM #

Test Results (last 3 years, if possible)

STATE ASSESSMENT FOR ELA* AND MATH	GRADES	GPA	HIGH SCHOOL EXIT EXAM RESULTS

*English language arts

The final section of the MLL shadowing profile is for the student's schedule so the educator knows where to find the MLL once he or she is at the school site. All of this information will be reviewed at the premeeting at the school on Day 2 of the shadowing training. Figure 6.8 is a completed MLL shadowing profile form that each participant will receive before shadowing an MLL on Day 2.

FIGURE 6.8   Completed MLL Student Profile for Shadowing

- Picture of MLL for visual identification

- **First name:** *Josue*
- **Date of birth:** *8/94*
- **Grade level:** *10*
- **Date of entry into United States:** *9/99*
- **Date of entry into district:** *9/99*

Classes or Periods to Be Shadowed

PERIOD/CLASS	COURSE TITLE	TEACHER	ROOM #
1	English 10P	Mr. Partridge	4A
2	Algebra 4	Mr. Gonzalez	113

(Continued)

FIGURE 6.8 (Continued)

Test Results (last 3 years, if possible)

ELPAC* OVERALL	LISTENING AND SPEAKING	READING	WRITING
Fall 2018: 4	4, 4	5	4
Fall 2019: 4	4, 4	3	4
Fall 2020: 4	4, 3	3	4

*English Language Proficiency Assessments for California

CAASPP* FOR ELA** AND MATH	GRADES	GPA	CAHSEE*** (HS ONLY)
ELA: 331	ELA: B	Total: 2.9091	ELA: Passed
Math: 279	Math: C	Academic: 2.8000	Math: Passed

*California Assessment of Student Performance and Progress

**English language arts

***California High School Exit Exam

Figure 6.8 contains the necessary information to both successfully shadow an MLL and analyze the MLL's progress during the debriefing session. It will be further explained in the section that follows.

DATA TALK FOR MLL SHADOWING DEBRIEFING

The MLL shadowing profile should also be analyzed again during the debriefing session of the MLL shadowing training in order to determine patterns and themes across all students and levels. The quantitative information—assessment data, grades, and GPA—can be compared against the qualitative data gathered via shadowing. Figure 6.9 shows the demographic information for Josue, along with a sample of the kind of analysis that should happen during the data talk portion of the debriefing session following the MLL shadowing experience.

According to the demographic data, Josue had been in the country for 11 years at the time of shadowing, with only 4 years of English language development progress. This makes Josue a long-term EL or LTEL, an MLL who has been in the country 6 years or more without reclassifying as fluent in English. The literature on LTELs tells us that Josue needs more academic

- Picture of MLL for visual identification

- **First name:** *Josue*
- **Date of birth:** *8/94*
- **Grade level:** *10*
- **Date of entry into United States:** *9/99*
- **Date of entry into district:** *9/99*

literacy development, which will grow out of the opportunities that educators provide for his oral language development.

Figure 6.10 shows Josue's English language proficiency scores for the past 3 years. The scores in Figure 6.10 demonstrate that Josue has not made progress on his overall scores over the past 3 years. Scores have remained the same at 4 for the past 3 years. It is important to note that on the ELPAC, students will receive an overall scale score and performance level consisting of oral language skills (speaking, listening) and written language skills (reading, writing). The four performance levels are 1 = Minimally Developed, 2 = Somewhat Developed, 3 = Moderately Developed, and 4 = Well Developed.

FIGURE 6.10 English Language Proficiency Scores

ENGLISH LANGUAGE PROFICIENCY ASSESSMENTS FOR CALIFORNIA (ELPAC*) SCORES OVERALL	LISTENING AND SPEAKING	READING	WRITING
Fall 2018: 4	*4, 4*	*5*	*4*
Fall 2019: 4	*4, 4*	*3*	*4*
Fall 2020: 4	*4, 3*	*3*	*4*

*English Language Proficiency Assessments for California

NOTE: The four performance levels are 1 = Minimally Developed, 2 = Somewhat Developed, 3 = Moderately Developed, and 4 = Well Developed.

After 11 years in the country, Josue should have already reclassified as fluent in English, according to both California state expectations (one language level per year) and second-language acquisition research (3 to 5 years overall for the social/basics of English; 5 to 7 years for academic English). Notice that Josue's listening scores have flatlined for the past 3 years and that he has regressed in speaking, as he has moved from 4 to 3. Similarly, Josue has regressed in reading by moving back two scores from 2018 to 2019 and maintaining that level in 2020. Josue has also flatlined in terms of his writing scores. These data show that after 11 years in the country, Josue needs more rigorous and structured academic oral language development opportunities, which can also lead to academic literacy development. More discussion on how to provide this kind of instruction will be discussed in Chapter 10.

ACADEMIC ACHIEVEMENT SCORES

Regarding academic achievement, Josue demonstrated below-grade-level assessment scores on the state assessment called the California Assessment of Student Performance and Progress (CAASPP), although he had passed the high school exit exam. The California High School Exit Exam (CAHSEE), however, only measures eighth-grade math and English skills. So although it is a positive indicator that Josue has passed the CAHSEE, he still has much more progress to make in terms of grade-level expectations. This is evident by Josue's grades and overall grade point average. When looking at Josue's strengths, we see that he is doing best in his Algebra II class, with a grade of an A–. This is an asset that should be built upon. Additionally, although Josue was receiving a B in English at the time of shadowing, he was taking a sheltered English course for MLLs. In a couple of years, when Josue enters college or the workplace, he will need much more than just basic English courses to succeed in college and beyond. Olsen, in *Reparable Harm* (2010), suggests that MLLs who have been in the country 6 years or more and are not making progress, as Josue is not, need specialized courses that will accelerate instruction while also teaching English, not further watering down of content. Such issues will be explored further in the debriefing section of the book. Figure 6.11 shows Josue's academic progress in English language arts (ELA) and mathematics.

FIGURE 6.11   MLL Achievement Data

GRADE-LEVEL CAASPP* SCORES FOR ELA AND MATH	GRADES	GPA	CAHSEE** (HS ONLY)
ELA: 1 (Standard Not Met)	ELA: B	Total: 2.9091	ELA: Passed
Math: 3 (Standard Met)	Math: A–	Academic: 2.8000	Math: Passed

*California Assessment of Student Performance and Progress

**California High School Exit Exam

As shown in Figure 6.11, Josue's GPA is just below a *C* average at 2.80, which does not seem so bad for an MLL. It is important to remember, however, that Josue is taking courses with below-grade-level expectations. For some schools in California, sheltered courses do count toward the *a–g* requirements (a set of required courses encompassing history, social science, lab science, English, math, foreign languages, arts, and college prep) needed for admission to the university system. The sheltered courses, which integrate language with content, taken in combination, will hardly prepare Josue for the kind of future that he deserves. If Josue wishes to attend college, these courses will not prepare him for the rigor and demands that he will encounter.

The MLL debriefing encourages a data talk similar to the one that has been written in this section, using the reflective questions included in the following section. The following section will also describe how to use the MLL shadowing information to further determine and focus on MLL needs systemically.

MLL SHADOWING PROTOCOL DATA TRIANGULATION

Student observation data regarding academic speaking and listening on the MLL Shadowing Protocol Form demonstrated that Josue had few opportunities for academic oral language development. Over the 2 hours that Josue was observed, he had only one opportunity for academic oral language development, which occurred in his first-period Algebra II class. This opportunity for academic speaking was not structured, so Josue only briefly took advantage of it. From the classroom observation data and Josue's achievement results, it is no wonder that Josue has actually regressed in speaking on the ELPAC, the language proficiency assessment, since he had almost no opportunities to speak in the two classrooms in which he was observed. In fact, Josue has regressed in speaking levels over the past 3 years by moving back from a Level 4 for 2 years to a Level 3 in his most recent assessment results for speaking. From these results, the educator might determine that more structured opportunities for classroom talk should be provided. Through a similar analysis, if this were true for most MLLs observed during the shadowing experience, then district or school efforts should be made toward training teachers to systemically embed academic oral language development in classrooms. An example of this can be found in Chapter 8 of the book.

The observation also demonstrated that although Josue tried intently to listen while in his English class, he often did not know what he was listening for, as he was not required or expected to listen specifically in the lesson design. Again, although Josue caused no behavioral issues in the classroom setting, he needed to know which portions of the lecture and video shown were important and which were not. In this way, he would have benefited from a graphic organizer that caused him to listen for key vocabulary or specific information. Additionally, if Josue struggled with listening in this way, then many more students could have as well. Training teachers around the different ways to structure listening for MLLs, as well as practical strategies for doing this, would prove helpful to many students to be actively engaged.

The poster shown in Figure 6.12 includes key questions that schools may consider as they review the data collected from the MLL shadowing experience. Once teachers have reflected on the trends and patterns from the MLL shadowing data, they can determine next steps that have been triangulated from both the achievement data and the classroom observations. This creates buy-in when new strategies or teaching methods are introduced so it no longer is a top-down approach to change.

FIGURE 6.12   MLL Shadowing Data Talk

MLL Data Talk

Tell your partner about your MLL:

- ELPAC scores (overall and by domain)
- ELA/math assessment scores
- Years in country/school

    ☐ Is the student progressing one language proficiency level per year on the ELPAC from when they arrived?

**What additional information did the shadowing observation give you about your student?

TARGETING PROFESSIONAL DEVELOPMENT ACCORDING TO MLL NEEDS

As participants in groups analyze data, as described previously, they will begin to see trends and themes regarding student needs. If the majority of MLLs at a particular school site have the same needs in terms of academic oral language development, then professional development should be targeted in that vein. As the MLL shadowing data collected are used in conjunction with student assessment data, the specific needs of this student group can be targeted. Since staff development data also tell us that teachers need at least 50 hours of professional development in a particular focus area to create change, it is important to follow-up shadowing by providing targeted professional development that will meet the needs of MLLs at each particular site. For example, if in the analysis it was found that most MLLs at a site were at the midrange of English language proficiency, with few systemic opportunities for academic oral language development, then teachers might want to begin to incorporate academic language stems, along with a content-area vocabulary word wall, in order to meet those language demands. MLLs at more midlevel and advanced levels of English language proficiency, with few opportunities for academic oral language development, might be ready for structured group work such as reciprocal teaching (more suggestions on next steps for professional development are presented in Chapter 10). In other words, the needs that emerge from the initial student assessment data, along with the aggregate trends of MLLs from the protocol site, should help direct and inform the professional development. The days of random, drive-by professional development are over in this time of intense student need and accountability. Such levels of data analysis, triangulated with classroom observation data from shadowing, should both create the level of urgency needed and create next steps. More information regarding follow-up trainings to shadowing will be addressed in subsequent chapters.

SCHOOL SITE MLL SHADOWING

When planning a school site MLL shadowing training, it is important to train all teachers with the Day 1 content in order to ensure that everyone is on the same page and has the same lens with which to observe students. At the school site, however, it is additionally important to make certain that a culture of trust and openness has already been set. If teachers are not used to being observed or having additional people in their classrooms, then MLL shadowing at one's own school site might not be the best option. If shadowing is completed at one's own site, the participant must be reminded that the shadowing training is about the experience of an MLL and not the teacher. Even so, teachers need to know that they will be in each other's classrooms, which often takes a level of trust for systems so that some of the results during the debriefing do not cause unnecessary alarm.

Once trust has been established at the school site level, it is important for organizers to conduct the same level of data analysis as suggested before—historical data on language proficiency assessments, state tests, as well as grades—for the level of MLL the system has determined that it would like to study. At the school site level, Day 1 of MLL shadowing can be conducted during district-allotted professional development days. Remember that it is not advisable to conduct an MLL shadowing training without first training teachers on the importance of academic speaking and active listening on Day 1. Once this is done, substitute teachers can be used to cover those teachers who are in classrooms shadowing on Day 2. Depending on the size of the faculty, substitutes can be obtained for half of the staff members in the morning, and then the other half of the staff members can shadow in the afternoon. In this scenario, it is important that all teachers receive the same full-day training on listening and speaking, as well as how to shadow, before going into classrooms to shadow on Day 2. Using this model, the members of one group (often half of the school site staff) can shadow for 2 hours and then spend 1 hour debriefing what they saw, as well as looking for themes and patterns in the observation, alongside the achievement data. The second group (the other half of the staff) can then do the same for the afternoon session. A more extensive debriefing, with data across both halves of the staff, can ensue when the staff members come together for their next faculty meeting. Figure 6.13 represents a schedule for MLL shadowing that can be used at a school site.

FIGURE 6.13   Shadowing School Site Schedule

SCHOOL SITE MLL SHADOWING MODEL	
DAY 1 **FULL- OR HALF-DAY PROFESSIONAL DEVELOPMENT**	**DAY 2** **HALF-DAY OBSERVATIONS WITH SUBS**
AM—Welcome and Agenda Review • Oral/Academic Language Development Overview • Break • Listening Overview PM—Shadowing Introduction • Practice With the Protocol • Day 2 Agenda Overview/Logistics/Student Profiles • Closing and Evaluations	AM—Brief Review of Protocol and MLL Profile (10–15 minutes) • MLL Shadowing in Classrooms (2 hours) • Debrief (45 minutes to 1 hour) **Repeat same schedule in PM with the rest of faculty.**

The schedule (Figure 6.13) can be modified for a full-day or half-day training session, depending on the amount of time available at the site. It is best to have a full day of training on Day 1 if at all possible, as many of the instructional strategies can be modeled and experienced only on the first day of the training. It is also important for all participants to become grounded in the MLL shadowing process so that they are comfortable using the protocol and coding student interactions on Day 2.

Figure 6.14 is an agenda for Day 2 of an MLL shadowing training at Dorothea Lange Elementary School in the Lucia Mar Unified School District in Arroyo Grande, California. At this school site, half of the faculty shadowed in the morning and the second half shadowed in the afternoon, with a whole-school debriefing at the end of the second day.

Additional MLL shadowing schedules will be presented in Chapter 10. The following chapter will demonstrate how to utilize specific components of the MLL shadowing protocol.

Lucia Mar Unified School District

Lange Elementary School

MLL Shadowing Agenda for May 9th

Group 1

8:30–8:55	MLL Shadowing Premeeting

- Distribute Student Profiles
- Reminders and Protocol Review

9:00–11:00	MLL Shadowing Observation in Classrooms
11:00–11:30	MLL Shadowing Mini Debriefing

Group 2

12:30–12:55	MLL Shadowing Premeeting

- Distribute Student Profiles
- Reminders and Protocol Review

1:00–3:00	MLL Shadowing Observation in Classrooms
3:00–3:30	MLL Shadowing Mini Debriefing
3:30-4:00	Whole-School Trends and Debriefing Patterns

REFERENCES

Gibbons, P. (2015). *Scaffolding language, scaffolding learning: Teaching second language learners in the mainstream classroom.* Portsmouth, NH: Heinemann.

Olsen, L. (2010). *Reparable harm: Fulfilling the unkept promise of educational opportunity for California's long-term English learners.* Long Beach, CA: Californians Together. Available at http://www.californianstogether.org/

CHAPTER 7

How to Use the Shadowing Protocol

So far, we have learned how to use the multilingual learner (MLL) shadowing protocol in order to collect data on academic speaking and listening. This chapter will focus on how to utilize all of the other components of the MLL shadowing protocol for classroom data collection. As a review, in using the MLL shadowing protocol, teachers should only monitor, at the start of every 5-minute interval, who the primary speaker is—either the student or teacher—as well as who the primary speaker is speaking to (see Chapter 4 for more on this). Educators should also remember that only *academic speaking* (not social talk) is to be noted and that only what is happening *first* at the start of the 5-minute interval should be listed. Any additional information after the start of the 5-minute interval can be listed under the comments section. Also, the types of listening involved in the interaction are monitored on the protocol, whether it is one way or two way. One-way listening is an interaction in which students take in information, such as a lecture. Two-way listening is when your MLL asks for clarification or engages in a dialogue. Figure 7.1 represents the four categories for listening that will be monitored using the MLL shadowing protocol.

Typically, in one-way listening, there is no room for clarification or questions. In contrast, two-way listening allows for clarification to be made, because the interaction is dialogue based. That is, the interaction is considered a conversation (see more about this in Chapter 5). Throughout the MLL shadowing project, participants are often astounded by the fact that the teacher will do most of the talking, with much of the interaction being lecture based, despite the fact that the MLLs need many opportunities to practice language in order to develop it.

FIGURE 7.1   Four Categories for Listening on Protocol

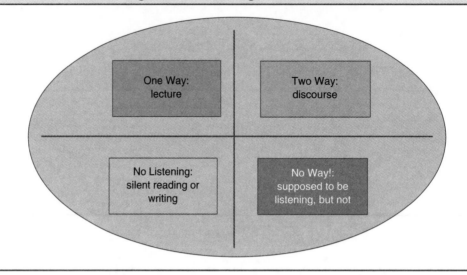

FIGURE 7.1   Four Categories for Listening on Protocol

SOURCE: Adapted from Gibbons (2015).

Figure 7.2 visually represents different examples and contexts in which students can listen.

FIGURE 7.2   Listening Contexts

	Two Way (Taking part in)		
Social	• A recess conversation about the rules for a game • Learning how to use the free lunch system • Planning for a holiday assembly	• A nutrition-break conversation about an upcoming assignment • Learning how to use the microscopes in science • Planning for a group presentation	**Academic**
	• Other students talking about their weekend fun • School announcements over the PA system • Schedule for bus pickups at the end of the day	• A read-aloud by the teacher • Directions from the teacher for writing a narrative account • Student-led small-group social studies presentation	
	One Way (Listening to)		

SOURCE: Adapted from Gibbons (2015).

It is important for educators to understand the listening contexts, as they will be monitoring them on the MLL shadowing protocol. Generally, participants need to understand that one-way listening is lecture based and two-way listening is dialogue based (for more on this, see Chapter 5, The Importance of Active Listening).

MLL SHADOWING PROTOCOL OVERVIEW

This section will explain step by step how to use each section of the protocol. Before actually shadowing an MLL, participants should be taught how to thoroughly use the protocol in advance of ever entering a classroom. This ensures that all educators have the same lens when they enter classrooms and are looking for the same evidence. Figure 7.3 is a blank MLL shadowing protocol. Each section of the protocol form will be explained in subsequent sections.

From Figure 7.3, it is evident that there are seven sections to the MLL shadowing protocol:

1. MLL student's demographic information (top portion of the protocol)

2. Time interval (noted at every 5 minutes)

3. Specific student activity to be taken down at the top of every 5-minute interval

4. Academic speaking codes/interactions

5. Academic listening codes/interactions

6. Coding for students who are not listening or required to listen

7. Comments section

Each of these sections will be explained thoroughly in the segments to follow.

FIGURE 7.3 Blank MLL Shadowing Protocol

Student: _____ School: _____ ELD Level: _____

Gender: _____ Grade Level: _____ Years in US Schools: _____ Years in District: _____

TIME	SPECIFIC STUDENT ACTIVITY/LOCATION OF STUDENT 5-MINUTE INTERVALS	ACADEMIC SPEAKING (CHECK ONE)	ACADEMIC LISTENING ONE WAY OR TWO WAY (CHECK ONE)	STUDENT IS NOT LISTENING (CHECK ONE)	COMMENTS
		□ Student to student—*1* □ Student to teacher—*2* □ Student to small group—*3* □ Student to whole class—*4* □ Teacher to student—*5* □ Teacher to small group—*6* □ Teacher to whole class—*7*	**One way or two way** □ Student listening mostly to student—*1* □ Student listening mostly to teacher—*2* □ Student listening mostly to small group—*3* □ Student listening mostly to whole class—*4*	□ Reading or writing silently—*1* □ Student is off task—*2*	
		□ Student to student—*1* □ Student to teacher—*2* □ Student to small group—*3* □ Student to whole class—*4* □ Teacher to student—*5* □ Teacher to small group—*6* □ Teacher to whole class—*7*	**One way or two way** □ Student listening mostly to student—*1* □ Student listening mostly to teacher—*2* □ Student listening mostly to small group—*3* □ Student listening mostly to whole class—*4*	□ Reading or writing silently—*1* □ Student is off task—*2*	

MLL DEMOGRAPHIC INFORMATION

The top portion, or the demographic information of the MLL shadowing protocol, should be filled out on the morning of Day 2 of the MLL shadowing training. This is when participants receive their MLL shadowing profile information. Schools or districts may also choose to pass out the MLL Profile Forms to participants at the end of Day 1 of the MLL shadowing training. If this is the case, then it is important to remind participants to bring their profile forms with them on Day 2 of the training. The demographic information on the protocol form includes the language proficiency level (ELD level in California schools), gender, and grade level, as well as years in U.S. schools and in the district. This information is important so that the participants know who they are shadowing so that they can properly analyze student data once they have completed their observations.

Figure 7.4 is the demographic section of the MLL Shadowing Form.

FIGURE 7.4 Demographic Information of MLL Shadowing Protocol

Student: _____   School: _____   ELD Level: _____

Gender: _____   Grade Level: _____   Years in US Schools: _____

Years in District: _____

MLLs who are shadowed should be selected according to the language proficiency level of the school site or district needed in order to analyze their academic speaking and listening experiences across an entire system. This information, then, also assists with next steps in determining and differentiating professional development at that specific level.

TRACKING TIME ON MLL SHADOWING PROTOCOL

The first column on the MLL shadowing protocol requires participants to write down the exact time of each interaction at every 5-minute interval (see Figure 7.5 highlighted).

In the first column, participants should note the exact time that they are recording their MLL's activities. This should then be done at every 5-minute interval from the first interaction recorded. That is, if the observation begins at 8:15 a.m., then the second interaction should be written at 8:20 a.m., and so on. This ensures that there is a pattern and consistency (or interrater reliability) in the way that student activities are recorded throughout the MLL shadowing observation. It is useful for the participants to have a watch or phone handy so that they can monitor time as accurately as possible. Classroom clocks are not always reliable or in working condition.

FIGURE 7.5 MLL Shadowing Protocol Highlighted for Time

TIME	SPECIFIC STUDENT ACTIVITY/ LOCATION OF STUDENT 5-MINUTE INTERVALS	ACADEMIC SPEAKING (CHECK ONE)	ACADEMIC LISTENING ONE WAY OR TWO WAY (CHECK ONE)	STUDENT IS NOT LISTENING (CHECK ONE)	COMMENTS
8:15		☐ Student to student—*1* ☐ Student to teacher—*2* ☐ Student to small group—*3* ☐ Student to whole class—*4* ☐ Teacher to student—*5* ☐ Teacher to small group—*6* ☐ Teacher to whole class—*7*	**One way or two way** ☐ Student listening mostly to student—*1* ☐ Student listening mostly to teacher—*2* ☐ Student listening mostly to small group—*3* ☐ Student listening mostly to whole class—*4*	☐ Reading or writing silently—*1* ☐ Student is off task—*2*	

TRACKING STUDENT ACTIVITIES ON MLL SHADOWING PROTOCOL

The second column on the MLL shadowing protocol requires participants to note the exact activity and location of the student and what is taking place at every 5-minute interval (see Figure 7.6 highlighted).

FIGURE 7.6 MLL Shadowing Protocol Highlighted for Student Activity

TIME	SPECIFIC STUDENT ACTIVITY/ LOCATION OF STUDENT 5-MINUTE INTERVALS	ACADEMIC SPEAKING (CHECK ONE)	ACADEMIC LISTENING ONE WAY OR TWO WAY (CHECK ONE)	STUDENT IS NOT LISTENING (CHECK ONE)	COMMENTS
	Josue completes his worksheet independently at his desk.	☐ Student to student—*1* ☐ Student to teacher—*2* ☐ Student to small group—*3* ☐ Student to whole class—*4* ☐ Teacher to student—*5* ☐ Teacher to small group—*6* ☐ Teacher to whole class—*7*	**One way or two way** ☐ Student listening mostly to student—*1* ☐ Student listening mostly to teacher—*2* ☐ Student listening mostly to small group—*3* ☐ Student listening mostly to whole class—*4*	☐ Reading or writing silently—*1* ☐ Student is off task—*2*	

In the second column, it is important that participants take down what their MLLs are doing at the top of every 5-minute interval only. That is, everything that is occurring during the entire 5-minute interval should not be taken down, as in a running record. Instead, for interrater reliability reasons, whatever activity the MLL is participating in *first* and *most* at the start of the 5-minute interval should be taken down. Any additional information regarding the 5-minute time period is then recorded in the last column called the comments section (more about this section in the paragraphs to come).

TRACKING ACADEMIC SPEAKING ON MLL SHADOWING PROTOCOL

The third column on the MLL shadowing protocol requires participants to take down who is doing the academic speaking—the MLL or the teacher—at the start of the 5-minute interval (see section highlighted in Figure 7.7).

FIGURE 7.7   MLL Shadowing Protocol Highlighted for Academic Speaking

TIME	SPECIFIC STUDENT ACTIVITY/ LOCATION OF STUDENT 5-MINUTE INTERVALS	ACADEMIC SPEAKING (CHECK ONE)	ACADEMIC LISTENING ONE WAY OR TWO WAY (CHECK ONE)	STUDENT IS NOT LISTENING (CHECK ONE)	COMMENTS
		☐ Student to student—**1** ☐ Student to teacher—**2** ☐ Student to small group—**3** ☐ Student to whole class—**4** ☐ Teacher to student—**5** ☐ Teacher to small group—**6** ☐ Teacher to whole class—**7**	**One way or two way** ☐ Student listening mostly to student—**1** ☐ Student listening mostly to teacher—**2** ☐ Student listening mostly to small group—**3** ☐ Student listening mostly to whole class—**4**	☐ Reading or writing silently—**1** ☐ Student is off task—**2**	

In the third column, notice that there is a section to check off the primary person speaking at the start of the 5-minute interval. Although the MLL shadowing observation is about the student, there is a section for teacher talk so that there is a way to take down data around who is talking *most* during the observation. In this way, note that by checking off boxes 1 through 4, participants are noting *student* talk.

Student speaking mostly to:

1. Another student (as in Think-Pair-Share)

2. Teacher (one-on-one conference or posing question)

3. Small group (as in reciprocal teaching)

4. Whole class (presenting to whole class)

Similarly, by checking off boxes 5 through 7, *teacher* talk is noted during the interaction. The teacher talk coding system was added to the MLL shadowing form in order to be able to code the segments of time when students were not speaking, as teacher talk was the most frequent occurrence of speaking when students were not speaking.

Teacher speaking mostly to:

5. Student (one-on-one conference or answering question)

6. Small group (small-group instruction or answering small-group question)

7. Whole class (lecture)

It is also important for participants to remember that only academic speaking experiences should be taken down. Social talk, such as friendly conversations or playground conversations, should not be coded as academic speaking. Instead, participants can make note of such interactions in the comments section of the observation form (to be discussed later). For more on the difference between academic and social speaking, see Chapter 4.

TRACKING ACADEMIC LISTENING ON MLL SHADOWING PROTOCOL

The fourth column on the MLL shadowing protocol, highlighted below, requires that participants record what kind of academic listening the student is experiencing—one way or two way—at the top of the 5-minute interval (see Figure 7.8 highlighted).

In the fourth column, participants are asked to check off the kind of listening that the MLL is engaged in at the top of the 5-minute interval. Notice that unlike the academic speaking column, participants are only checking off to whom the student is listening most. In this section, we are not recording what the teacher is doing at all. There are four coding options here:

1. Student listening mostly to a student (as in Think-Pair-Share)

2. Student listening mostly to a teacher (as in a lecture)

3. Student listening mostly to a small group (as in reciprocal teaching)

4. Student listening mostly to the whole class (as in choral reading or singing)

For more information on the contexts and kinds of listening (academic or social), see Chapter 5.

FIGURE 7.8 MLL Shadowing Protocol Highlighted for Academic Listening

TIME	SPECIFIC STUDENT ACTIVITY/ LOCATION OF STUDENT 5-MINUTE INTERVALS	ACADEMIC SPEAKING (CHECK ONE)	ACADEMIC LISTENING ONE WAY OR TWO WAY (CHECK ONE)	STUDENT IS NOT LISTENING (CHECK ONE)	COMMENTS
		☐ Student to student—*1* ☐ Student to teacher—*2* ☐ Student to small group—*3* ☐ Student to whole class—*4* ☐ Teacher to student—*5* ☐ Teacher to small group—*6* ☐ Teacher to whole class—*7*	**One way or two way** ☐ Student listening mostly to student—*1* ☐ Student listening mostly to teacher—*2* ☐ Student listening mostly to small group—*3* ☐ Student listening mostly to whole class—*4*	☐ Reading or writing silently—*1* ☐ Student is off task—*2*	

TRACKING STUDENTS NOT LISTENING OR NOT REQUIRED TO LISTEN ON THE MLL SHADOWING PROTOCOL

The fifth column on the MLL shadowing protocol requires participants to take down occurrences when students are not listening or are not required to listen (see Figure 7.9 highlighted).

In the fifth column, participants have two options that should only be checked off when appropriate. The first box can be checked off when students are not listening, but they *should* be listening. This includes off-task behavior of any kind. The second box can be checked off when MLLs *are not* specifically required to listen but are not off task. Examples of this include when students are required to read or write silently. This option is made available so that independent work and off-task behavior can be appropriately coded.

TIME	SPECIFIC STUDENT ACTIVITY/ LOCATION OF STUDENT 5-MINUTE INTERVALS	ACADEMIC SPEAKING (CHECK ONE)	ACADEMIC LISTENING ONE WAY OR TWO WAY (CHECK ONE)	STUDENT IS NOT LISTENING (CHECK ONE)	COMMENTS
		☐ Student to student—*1* ☐ Student to teacher—*2* ☐ Student to small group—*3* ☐ Student to whole class—*4* ☐ Teacher to student—*5* ☐ Teacher to small group—*6* ☐ Teacher to whole class—*7*	**One way or two way** ☐ Student listening mostly to student—*1* ☐ Student listening mostly to teacher—*2* ☐ Student listening mostly to small group—*3* ☐ Student listening mostly to whole class—*4*	☐ Reading or writing silently—*1* ☐ Student is off task—*2*	

TRACKING COMMENTS ON THE MLL SHADOWING PROTOCOL

The sixth column on the MLL shadowing protocol requires participants to record comments (see Figure 7.10 highlighted).

FIGURE 7.10   MLL Shadowing Protocol Highlighted for Comments

TIME	SPECIFIC STUDENT ACTIVITY/ LOCATION OF STUDENT 5-MINUTE INTERVALS	ACADEMIC SPEAKING (CHECK ONE)	ACADEMIC LISTENING ONE WAY OR TWO WAY (CHECK ONE)	STUDENT IS NOT LISTENING (CHECK ONE)	COMMENTS
		☐ Student to student—*1* ☐ Student to teacher—*2* ☐ Student to small group—*3* ☐ Student to whole class—*4* ☐ Teacher to student—*5* ☐ Teacher to small group—*6* ☐ Teacher to whole class—*7*	**One way or two way** ☐ Student listening mostly to student—*1* ☐ Student listening mostly to teacher—*2* ☐ Student listening mostly to small group—*3* ☐ Student listening mostly to whole class—*4*	☐ Reading or writing silently—*1* ☐ Student is off task—*2*	

In the sixth column, participants take down additional comments that will be helpful in analyzing interactions once the observation is completed. Additional comments may include explanations that further clarify the activity that the MLL participated in or information regarding interactions that are unclear to the observer. Additionally, participants can take down comments that explain what occurred during the rest of the 5-minute interval, which may not have been noted in the first column regarding the primary activity. The information in the comments section will later be analyzed for themes and patterns and provides important reasons why the specific phenomenon or activity may be occurring in the classroom setting.

COMPLETED MLL SHADOWING PROTOCOL

Figure 7.11 demonstrates how to complete the MLL shadowing protocol, using examples of the kinds of interactions that might occur in the classroom setting. Below is a protocol that has been coded for a quick write.

FIGURE 7.11 MLL Shadowing Protocol With Quick-Write Example

Student: *Josue*		**School:** *Si Se Puede High School*		**ELD Level: Level 4**— *Early Advanced*	
Gender: *Male*		**Grade Level:** *10*	**Years in US Schools:** *11 years*	**Years in District:** *11 years*	
TIME	**SPECIFIC STUDENT ACTIVITY/ LOCATION OF STUDENT 5-MINUTE INTERVALS**	**ACADEMIC SPEAKING (CHECK ONE)**	**ACADEMIC LISTENING ONE WAY OR TWO WAY (CHECK ONE)**	**STUDENT IS NOT LISTENING (CHECK ONE)**	**COMMENTS**
8:00 a.m.	*Student participates in quick write regarding prompt, "What impacted you most about yesterday's reading?"*	☐ Student to student—**1** ☐ Student to teacher—**2** ☐ Student to small group—**3** ☐ Student to whole class—**4** ☐ Teacher to student—**5** ☐ Teacher to small group—**6** ☐ Teacher to whole class—**7**	**One way or two way** ☐ Student listening mostly to student—**1** ☐ Student listening mostly to teacher—**2** ☐ Student listening mostly to small group—**3** ☐ Student listening mostly to whole class—**4**	☑ Reading or writing silently—**1** ☐ Student is off task—**2**	*Josue starts on task with writing, but doesn't seem to write very much. It seems like he could use some help to stay on task.*

Notice in the first column that the exact time—8:00 a.m.—has been recorded. In the second column, the activity, a quick write, and the exact prompt, have been taken down. The quick-write example has been coded in the fifth column, which allows participants to track occurrences when MLLs are not required to listen or are not listening. In this case, Josue is asked to respond to a writing prompt regarding material presented the day before, which does not require him to speak or listen. Notice that in the final column, additional details about his actions—that Josue starts off strong, tapers off, and could use some help—have been recorded. The comments section is the place where any anecdotal information should be noted. It is important to take down the comments section information carefully, as it will often explain *why* the MLL is not engaging or interacting as we would like. As we analyze themes and trends from the comments section in the debriefing section, we can often determine additional instructional needs that the MLLs shadowed might have. The next few sets of examples will explain how several additional classroom situations should be coded.

CODING FOR THINK-PAIR-SHARE

Figure 7.12 demonstrates how a Think-Pair-Share exchange should be coded.

FIGURE 7.12   MLL Shadowing Protocol With Think-Pair-Share

Student: *Josue*		**School:** *Si Se Puede High School*			**LD Level: Level 4**—*Early Advanced*
Gender: *Male*		**Grade Level:** *10*	**Years in US Schools:** *11 years*		**Years in District:** *11 years*

TIME	SPECIFIC STUDENT ACTIVITY/ LOCATION OF STUDENT 5-MINUTE INTERVALS	ACADEMIC SPEAKING (CHECK ONE)	ACADEMIC LISTENING ONE WAY OR TWO WAY (CHECK ONE)	STUDENT IS NOT LISTENING (CHECK ONE)	COMMENTS
8:05 a.m.	Josue shares his quick-write prompt with his partner via Think-Pair-Share.	☑ Student to student—**1** ☐ Student to teacher—**2** ☐ Student to small group—**3** ☐ Student to whole class—**4** ☐ Teacher to student—**5** ☐ Teacher to small group—**6** ☐ Teacher to whole class—**7**	**One way or two way** ☐ Student listening mostly to student—**1** ☐ Student listening mostly to teacher—**2** ☐ Student listening mostly to small group—**3** ☐ Student listening mostly to whole class—**4**	☐ Reading or writing silently—**1** ☐ Student is off task—**2**	Josue shares well and seems to stay on task with his conversation due to the sentence starter provided by the teacher.

In the first column, note the next 5-minute interval from the quick write—8:05 a.m.—has been taken down. Additionally, in the second column, the primary activity of Think-Pair-Share has been documented. Josue is now being asked to discuss his quick-write prompt, or what he learned from yesterday's class session, with the partner sitting next to him. Because he is talking to another student, this has been coded a 1 (student to student) for academic speaking. The comments section indicates that he is able to stay on task because of the sentence starter provided to him by the teacher. This is helpful information for teachers, as it demonstrates a scaffolding strategy that is helpful to Josue and perhaps other MLLs.

CODING FOR TEACHER LECTURE

Figure 7.13 demonstrates how a teacher lecture, or a time when the teacher is doing most of the talking, should be coded. Note that this has been coded for a 15-minute time segment.

FIGURE 7.13   MLL Shadowing Protocol With Teacher Lecture

Student: *Josue*		**School:** *Si Se Puede High School*			**ELD Level:** *Level 4—Early Advanced*
Gender: *Male*		**Grade Level:** *10*	**Years in US Schools:** *11 years*		**Years in District:** *11 years*
TIME	**SPECIFIC STUDENT ACTIVITY/ LOCATION OF STUDENT 5-MINUTE INTERVALS**	**ACADEMIC SPEAKING (CHECK ONE)**	**ACADEMIC LISTENING ONE WAY OR TWO WAY (CHECK ONE)**	**STUDENT IS NOT LISTENING (CHECK ONE)**	**COMMENTS**
8:10 a.m.	The teacher gives general directions for the next group activity, which will be reciprocal teaching, based on the reading completed the day before.	☐ Student to student—*1* ☐ Student to teacher—*2* ☐ Student to small group—*3* ☐ Student to whole class—*4* ☐ Teacher to student—*5* ☐ Teacher to small group—*6* ☑ Teacher to whole class—*7*	**One way or two way** ☐ Student listening mostly to student—*1* ☑ Student listening mostly to teacher—*2* ☐ Student listening mostly to small group—*3* ☐ Student listening mostly to whole class—*4*	☐ Reading or writing silently—*1* ☐ Student is off task—*2*	The teacher explains how students will use the reading from the previous day's class session to complete a group activity called reciprocal teaching. Josue seems to be excited about working in a group and listens for his role. In Spanish, he tells his friend that he wants to be the connector.
8:15 a.m.	The teacher explains each role associated with reciprocal teaching and how to complete it.	☐ Student to student—*1* ☐ Student to teacher—*2* ☐ Student to small group—*3* ☐ Student to whole class—*4* ☐ Teacher to student—*5* ☐ Teacher to small group—*6* ☑ Teacher to whole class—*7*	**One way or two way** ☐ Student listening mostly to student—*1* ☑ Student listening mostly to teacher—*2* ☐ Student listening mostly to small group—*3* ☐ Student listening mostly to whole class—*4*	☐ Reading or writing silently—*1* ☐ Student is off task—*2*	Josue seems to be a bit off task during this segment of the directions. He could use some structure for listening here. Maybe require notes on graphic organizer?

(Continued)

FIGURE 7.13 (Continued)

TIME	SPECIFIC STUDENT ACTIVITY/ LOCATION OF STUDENT 5-MINUTE INTERVALS	ACADEMIC SPEAKING (CHECK ONE)	ACADEMIC LISTENING ONE WAY OR TWO WAY (CHECK ONE)	STUDENT IS NOT LISTENING (CHECK ONE)	COMMENTS
8:20 a.m.	*The teacher assigns specific roles associated with reciprocal teaching to each student.*	☐ Student to student—**1** ☐ Student to teacher—**2** ☐ Student to small group—**3** ☐ Student to whole class—**4** ☐ Teacher to student—**5** ☐ Teacher to small group—**6** ☑ Teacher to whole class—**7**	**One way or two way** ☐ Student listening mostly to student—**1** ☑ Student listening mostly to teacher—**2** ☐ Student listening mostly to small group—**3** ☐ Student listening mostly to whole class—**4**	☐ Reading or writing silently—**1** ☐ Student is off task—**2**	*Josue seems to be listening intently again for what his role will be. He is happy to find out that he will be the connector.*

At 8:10 a.m., the teacher gives general directions to the whole class regarding how they will use the class reading from the past few days in order to complete a group activity. The third column has been coded a 7 because the teacher is talking to the whole class. Additionally, the fourth column has been coded a 2 because Josue is listening to the teacher, as the comments also suggest. He is briefly heard telling his neighbor in Spanish that he wants to be the connector, which has been taken down in the comments section. He seems to be excited about working on a group activity.

At 8:15 a.m., the teacher begins to explain the specifics of how reciprocal teaching works, including each of the four distinctive roles: summarizer, questioner, predictor, and connector. The teacher explains how each role should be completed and passes out the graphic organizer for students to review. Since the teacher is doing most of the talking here, the third column is coded a 7. In the comments section, it has been noted that perhaps the teacher could have had all students, including Josue, take notes on the graphic organizer regarding each of the roles.

At 8:20 a.m., the teacher assigns an individual role to each student. Josue seems to be listening intently again for his role to be called out, so the fourth column is coded a 2 (listening mostly to the teacher). Since the teacher is still talking, the third column has been coded a 7 (teacher talking to whole class). Notice that additional comments have been recorded in the final column, including how Josue cheers when he finds out that he has been assigned the connector role.

CODING FOR GROUP WORK

Figure 7.14 demonstrates how group work, like reciprocal teaching, should be coded. Notice again that this has been coded for a 15-minute segment.

FIGURE 7.14 MLL Shadowing Protocol With Group Work

Student: *Josue* **School:** *Si Se Puede High School* **ELD Level:** *Level 4—Early Advanced*

Gender: *Male* **Grade Level:** *10* **Years in US Schools:** *11 years* **Years in District:** *11 years*

TIME	SPECIFIC STUDENT ACTIVITY/LOCATION OF STUDENT 5-MINUTE INTERVALS	ACADEMIC SPEAKING (CHECK ONE)	ACADEMIC LISTENING ONE WAY OR TWO WAY (CHECK ONE)	STUDENT IS NOT LISTENING (CHECK ONE)	COMMENTS
8:25 a.m.	Josue listens as his team members review each of their roles.	☐ Student to student—**1** ☐ Student to teacher—**2** ☐ Student to small group—**3** ☐ Student to whole class—**4** ☐ Teacher to student—**5** ☐ Teacher to small group—**6** ☐ Teacher to whole class—**7**	**One way or two way** ☐ Student listening mostly to student—**1** ☐ Student listening mostly to teacher—**2** ☑ Student listening mostly to small group—**3** ☐ Student listening mostly to whole class—**4**	☐ Reading or writing silently—**1** ☐ Student is off task—**2**	Josue moves his desk so that he is situated with his group members. He listens intently to his group members' plans.
8:30 a.m.	Josue independently completes his connector role.	☐ Student to student—**1** ☐ Student to teacher—**2** ☐ Student to small group—**3** ☐ Student to whole class—**4** ☐ Teacher to student—**5** ☐ Teacher to small group—**6** ☐ Teacher to whole class—**7**	**One way or two way** ☐ Student listening mostly to student—**1** ☐ Student listening mostly to teacher—**2** ☐ Student listening mostly to small group—**3** ☐ Student listening mostly to whole class—**4**	☐ Reading or writing silently—**1** ☐ Student is off task—**2**	Josue takes out his reading materials from the day before. He works well the entire 5-minute interval.
8:35 a.m.	Josue begins to share his connector role with the rest of his group.	☐ Student to student—**1** ☐ Student to teacher—**2** ☐ Student to small group—**3** ☑ Student to whole class—**4** ☐ Teacher to student—**5** ☐ Teacher to small group—**6** ☐ Teacher to whole class—**7**	**One way or two way** ☐ Student listening mostly to student—**1** ☐ Student listening mostly to teacher—**2** ☐ Student listening mostly to small group—**3** ☐ Student listening mostly to whole class—**4**	☐ Reading or writing silently—**1** ☐ Student is off task—**2**	Josue gets to speak! He seems to be interested because he got the group role he wanted. The rest of his group tries to support him.

At 8:25 a.m., Josue listens to his group members as they review the role that each person will be completing. Note that since Josue and the teacher are not the ones speaking, the third column has been left blank. Since Josue is listening, however, the fourth column has been coded a 3, as he listens to his group members intently. The comments section describes the interaction further.

At 8:30 a.m., Josue independently works on his reciprocal teaching role of connector, which has been coded a 2 (student reads or writes silently) in the fifth column. Notice that the comments section describes him as conscientiously taking out his materials and working through the entire 5-minute interval. At 8:35 a.m., Josue gets his first opportunity to talk to his small group regarding his group role. This exchange has been coded a 3 (student talking to a small group) in the third column. The comments section suggests that Josue has a caring and supportive group and that it encourages him when needed.

CONTINUED CODING

During an MLL shadowing, educators would continue to code interactions in this manner at every 5-minute interval, for 2 hours or up to 4 hours. As demonstrated in the previous 5-minute intervals, the shadowing project allows educators to begin to find patterns regarding who is doing most of the speaking in classrooms and what kinds of listening MLLs are often asked to undertake. Educators soon begin to notice that the primary speaker in classrooms is often the teacher, which was true for Josue in the previous example. In fact, in this example, Josue only received one opportunity to speak. Similarly, educators find that the listening interactions are often one way, or in lecture mode, with little room for questions or clarification on the part of the MLL. Again, this was Josue's experience in the examples noted throughout this chapter.

In the shadowing debriefing process, analyzing these student interactions across participants becomes essential in changing instructional practices systemically (see Chapter 8). Similarly, the shadowing project illuminates for teachers how the absence of opportunities for academic speaking impacts MLL achievement. Through this process, educators are able to reflect on their own instructional practices, as well as how such practices may positively or negatively impact student achievement. For example, one teacher in the Los Angeles Unified School District's (LAUSD) District 6 stated, "The person talking most is the person who is learning most . . . and I'm doing most of the talking in my class!" This process, then, creates the urgency for beginning to change instructional practice systematically across levels. In this way, teachers begin to see *why* they need to change their instructional practices in order to make more room for student talk in the classroom setting. From the MLL shadowing experience, it is often teachers who want to take the lead around eliciting more talk across a school day. From this experience, the results and next steps should immediately be analyzed and leveraged in order to bring about change for MLLs.

MLL SHADOWING APP

In 2014, through generous grant funding from the California Community Foundation (CCF), colleague Linda Meyer and I were able to develop the MLL Shadowing app. The app was then piloted for 2 years as part of the CCF grant work within a local district. This section will summarize the features of the app, which is available as part of MLL professional development through the author.

Before the shadowing observation, unique IDs are assigned to each school and observer to ensure confidentiality is maintained. Observers are also instructed not to enter personally identifiable information into the app. Figure 7.15 demonstrates how observers enter observation and school IDs for confidentiality.

FIGURE 7.15 MLL App IDs

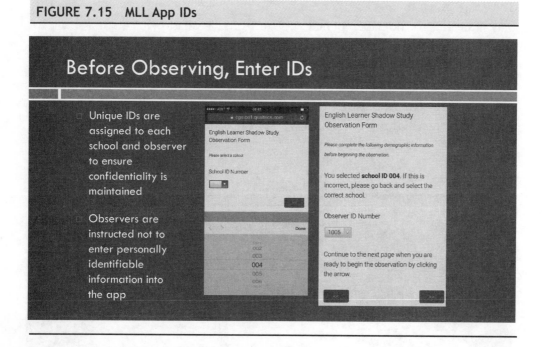

The MLL app also mirrors the paper-pencil version of the MLL shadowing protocol. The app has a clean display and prompts the observer to take down data at every 5-minute interval. The same fields are completed for each interval, and the drop-down menus assist with ensuring accuracy in coding. Figure 7.16 shows the clean display of the MLL Shadowing app.

FIGURE 7.16 MLL Shadowing Display

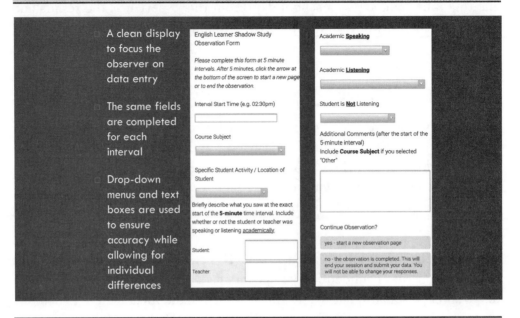

The drop-down menus are then tapped to display choices. Notice that the display is similar to the paper-pencil version of MLL shadowing with a space for time. The internal clock within the app actually monitors and reminds observers of the 5-minute interval. There are then drop-down menus for the course subject of the observation, as well as the specific student activity and location of the student. There is also a drop-down menu for the coding of the activity. Figure 7.17 highlights the drop-down features.

FIGURE 7.17 Drop-Down Features of MLL Shadowing App

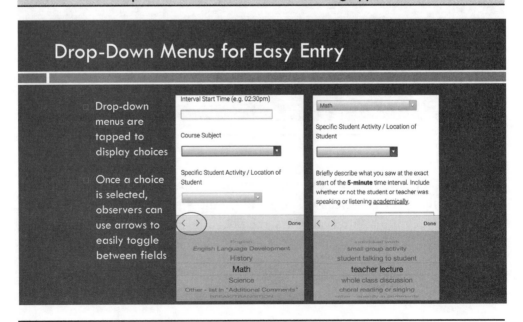

The MLL Shadowing app also includes drop-down menus for user-friendly coding of academic speaking, listening, and not listening at each 5-minute interval. The same seven options for academic speaking in the paper-pencil version are included in the app, and the same four options for academic listening are included in the app. Figure 7.18 shows the drop-down menus for coding and easy entry.

FIGURE 7.18   MLL App Coding for Easy Entry

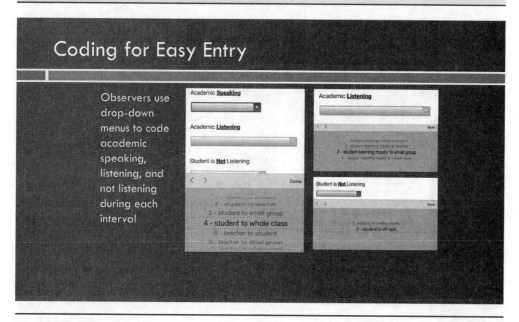

Text boxes in the app mirror the paper-pencil comments section. Here, observers can describe what their students are doing in more detail during each 5-minute interval. Observers are also prompted to complete each text box to ensure complete and accurate data are collected for analysis at the end. Figure 7.19 demonstrates how the text boxes can be used to take down specific comments while observing.

FIGURE 7.19   Text Boxes for Comments

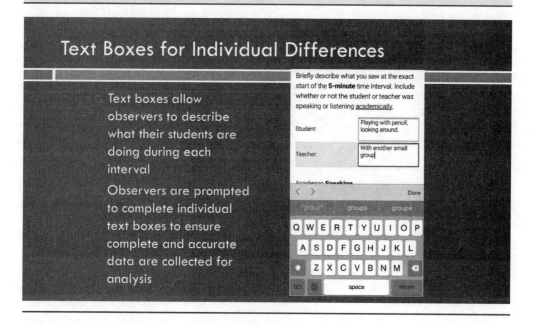

Lastly, the MLL Shadowing app is able to calculate how many intervals were coded and displays the summary at the end of the observation. The app will make these calculations for student academic speaking, teacher academic speaking, student academic listening, and student not listening. These data can then be used for future goal-setting and planning purposes. Figure 7.20 is a sample data summary display.

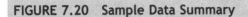

FIGURE 7.20   Sample Data Summary

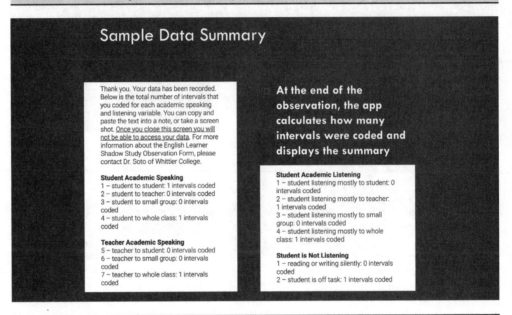

For more information about the MLL Shadowing app, contact Dr. Ivannia Soto at Whittier College.

References

Gibbons, P. (2015). *Scaffolding language, scaffolding learning: Teaching second language learners in the mainstream classroom.* Portsmouth, NH: Heinemann.

Meyer, L. (2014). *MLL Shadowing app.* Whittier, CA: Whittier College.

SECTION IV

Debriefing the Shadowing Experience

CHAPTER 8

Analyzing and Reflecting on the Results of Shadowing

DEBRIEFING THE MLL SHADOWING EXPERIENCE

Once the data on academic speaking and listening have been captured individually, an aggregate of the multilingual learner (MLL) shadowing experience is taken, either by level (elementary, middle, or high school), school site (if shadowing occurred at multiple school sites), or both by tallying responses by mode for academic speaking and listening. The aggregate then identifies the need that students have regarding the role of academic speaking and listening at each site or level. Additionally, the aggregate should identify professional development needs at each site or level. The power of MLL shadowing comes both from the classroom observation itself and from the follow-up discussions and plans that occur as a result of the experience. It is important to remember that MLL shadowing is not a panacea. It is a way to create change across a system when specific planning and follow-up are completed after the MLL shadowing experience. The aggregate numbers from shadowing allow participants to quantify what they just saw happening with their own MLL. That is, unfortunately, many MLLs often experience the fate of spending less than 2% or even 5–10% of their school day in academic oral language development. When this phenomenon is experienced both by the individual and by groups of educators, the urgency around the systemic need and change required becomes palpable. Groups of educators almost never want to turn away without doing something to effect change.

There are four steps to the MLL shadowing debriefing session on Day 2 of the training:

1. MLL shadowing reflection process
2. Tallying of academic speaking and listening
3. Two-word response analysis
4. MLL data talk triangulation of data

The following section will explain each of those processes.

MLL SHADOWING REFLECTION

The MLL shadowing debriefing session begins with the MLL Shadowing Experience: Reflection form, part of which is shown in Figure 8.1 (for the full form, see Appendix A, page 142, or http://www.corwin.com/MLLshadowing). This reflection process includes a series of questions that allow the participants to think about what they just experienced when shadowing their MLLs. These questions also allow participants to go back to the Gibbons materials from Day 1 of the training and to reflect on some of the changes that they might want to adopt systematically at their own sites. The MLL shadowing reflection questions begin individually and then move out toward finding themes and patterns across participants. Notice each of the questions in Figure 8.1, which are explained in detail in subsequent paragraphs.

FIGURE 8.1 MLL Shadowing Experience: Reflection

1. Write a short reflection on your observation of the student's learning experience.
2. Share your written experience with a partner. Identify common elements.
3. As a group of three or more, identify common elements. Select someone at your table to share common elements with the entire group.
4. Review "Looking at Classroom Talk" in Gibbons (2015), pp. 17–18. Think about your student. Think about _____ (name of student). Did you observe your student in any group work?
5. If the eight characteristics were in place within each classroom, would the observation experience have been the same?

Figure 8.1 demonstrates the first set of questions that participants will use to debrief the MLL shadowing experience. The five questions are important for the following reasons:

1. Write a short reflection on your observation of the student's learning experience. This question is completed individually by each participant. Participants should be instructed to write down key impressions regarding what they just experienced with MLL shadowing. I often ask participants to think about what the MLL himself or herself might say about what school was like as participants observed. If participants choose this route for their reflection, they do not have to write with an MLL's voice or in the first person. This is just a way for participants, if they are struggling with how to do it, to describe their MLL's experience in school. These reflections can come from either the quantitative (coding) or the qualitative (comments) sections of the MLL shadowing observation form.

2. Share your written experience with a partner. Identify common elements. Participants turn and talk to a partner regarding what they experienced with their own MLL. Commonalities, themes, and patterns, between both participants, should be taken down for this question. If there are only differences between the two experiences, partners should record them and note them as such.

3. As a group of three or more, identify common elements. Select someone at your table to share common elements with the entire group. This question can be completed by three participants at a table or with the entire group. Participants can summarize commonalities at each table and then have one person share them with the entire group. This allows participants to further see that across grades or levels, there are patterns of needs that should be addressed.

4. Review "Looking at Classroom Talk" (Gibbons [2015], pp. 17–18). Think about your student. Think about _____ (name of student). Did you observe your student in any group work? This question allows participants to go back into Gibbons's work from Day 1 of the training and think through the benefits of student talk for MLLs. Participants can note exactly what kind of group work students were engaged in if the participants saw it taking place. If no group work was observed, participants can reflect on how their MLLs *would have* benefited had group work been available.

5. If the eight characteristics (see Figure 8.2) were in place within each classroom, would the observation experience have been the same? The final question connects participants with the Eight Characteristics of Productive Group Work from Gibbons's work (which is shown in Figure 8.2), presented on Day 1 of the training.

FIGURE 8.2 Eight Characteristics of Productive Group Work for MLL Students

1. Clear and explicit instructions are provided.
2. Talk is necessary for the task.
3. There is a clear outcome.
4. The task is cognitively appropriate.
5. The task is integrated with a broader topic.
6. All children are involved.
7. Students have enough time.
8. Students know how to work in groups.

SOURCE: Adapted from Gibbons (2015).

Participants should document any of the eight characteristics of productive group work introduced on Day 1 of the training if they were observed in the classroom setting. If these characteristics were not observed, participants should note how the MLL's experience *could have* been enhanced as a result of the characteristics. It is important to remember that part of the answer to the lack of academic speaking experiences encountered by MLLs comes from ensuring that group work is used to elicit more language and that group work is structured so it can be productive and effective.

TWO-WORD RESPONSE SUMMARY

Once the MLL shadowing experience reflection form has been completed and reviewed by the group, participants should be asked to synthesize their MLL's overall experience using two adjectives that can be written at the top of their reflection form. Participants are then asked to share one word with the entire group while someone writes them on poster paper or on a whiteboard. Any words that are duplicated should be tallied. For example, during MLL shadowing trainings, I often hear the words *invisible* and *silent* used to describe what was experienced regarding an MLL's day in school. For the participants, the process of hearing these words out loud further makes concrete that the needs of MLLs are vast and that we all must do something about them. Figure 8.3 is the MLL Shadowing wordle that was created from the two-word response at the Sonoma County Office of Education training. You'll notice that many of the words are quite sobering. Collecting these words allows educators to visually see the impact of the aggregate MLL shadowing qualitative data.

FIGURE 8.3 Two-Word MLL Shadowing Wordle

SOURCE: Created at wordle.net

The power of seeing, in two descriptive words, that the needs of MLLs were so similar and common further solidifies for the group the consciousness around the next steps that must be taken in order to change instruction systemically. Organizers of the training may also ask participants to write their words on sticky notes, which can then be sorted into commonalities. It is still encouraged that participants read their words out loud before placing them on posters so that everyone hears the power of the words that have described the MLL's experience. Commonalities can then be shared with the organizers of the training in order to emphasize the patterns and themes emerging. Figure 8.4 provides the step-by-step directions for the two-word response process.

FIGURE 8.4 Two-Word Shadowing Synthesis

- Select two words to describe your MLL's experience in school today.
- Share your two words with your group and tally any words that were found in common.
- As an entire group, share the commonalities that were found within each small group.

MLL DATA TALK

After the two-word MLL shadowing synthesis is completed, the MLL data talk should be used. This process allows participants to triangulate the achievement data provided for their MLL student with the classroom observations collected. Since participants have already reviewed their MLL's achievement data before they observed the student, they should now look for possible reasons for the achievement progress—or lack of progress—from what they saw in the classroom. For example, if it was discovered that the MLL had very few academic speaking opportunities, then participants can begin to discuss how structuring Think-Pair-Share or having more productive group-work opportunities would elicit more consistent academic speaking in the classroom setting. Figure 8.5 outlines the way the MLL data talk session should be structured using the Think-Pair-Share structure.

FIGURE 8.5 MLL Data Talk

Tell Your Partner About Your MLL

- Language Proficiency Assessment scores (overall and by domain)
- State Achievement Scores (ELA and Math)
- Years in country/school
  - o Is the student progressing one level per year on the language proficiency level from when he or she arrived?

What additional information did the shadowing observation give you about your student?

Participants should be instructed to turn to a table partner and interview him or her regarding the MLL shadowed. They should pay careful attention to the following details:

- English language proficiency scores: The state English language proficiency scores should be analyzed, both year by year for the past 3 years and for each literacy domain (in California, these scores are given for listening, speaking, reading, and writing, as well as an overall score). Participants should pay careful attention to see if their MLL has progressed one level per year in each of the domains of language. These scores can then be compared to the progress being made in grades in the MLL's English language development course, as well as the classroom observation of that course, if participants shadowed there.

- State assessment results: The state grade-level assessment should similarly be analyzed for year-to-year progress. It should be noted if MLLs are making progress each year or regressing in achievement. These scores can then be compared to the progress the MLL is making in his or her math and English courses, as well as the classroom observation of that course if participants shadowed there.

- Years in country: Participants should carefully note the number of years their MLL has been in school compared to the level of progress that the student has been making since first coming into the United States. Both second-language theorists and the U.S. Department of Education would like MLLs to progress one level per year.

- Additional information: Any additional information, including information recorded in the comments section, should be discussed here. For example, if the MLL seemed tired or off task or on task and resilient, that information should be noted here.

The achievement data information should then be triangulated with the classroom observation data collected. This process should provide reasons certain achievement results might be occurring. For example, if your MLL has not been making progress in listening on the language proficiency assessment, perhaps the student was also struggling to pay attention in the classes in which he or she was observed. Such information will assist with recommendations and next steps for the MLL in the future.

TALLY RESPONSES

The final step in the MLL shadowing debriefing session should be to tally the number of responses for the academic speaking, listening, no/not listening, and comments sections of the MLL shadowing protocol (see Figure 8.6). The following section describes what participants should do as they tally the responses that were taken down during the MLL shadowing observation.

FIGURE 8.6 Tallying Responses

- Count up each of the Academic Speaking and Academic Listening components.
  - Tally the results on the poster.
- Synthesize your comments onto two sticky notes.

Participants should go through each of their MLL shadowing forms and complete the following for each section:

1. **Academic speaking:** Participants should count the number of 1 (student to student), 2 (student to teacher), 3 (student to small group), 4 (student to whole class), 5 (teacher to student), 6 (teacher to small group), and 7 (teacher to whole class) boxes that were checked off.

2. **Academic listening:** Count the number of 1 (student to student), 2 (student to teacher), 3 (student to small group), and 4 (student to whole class) boxes that were checked off.

3. **Student not listening/no listening:** Count the number of 1 (reading or writing silently) and 2 (student not listening) boxes that were checked off.

4. **Comments:** Participants should summarize all of their comments from the comments section on two sticky notes.

The MLL Shadowing Protocol in Figure 8.7 demonstrates how items can be tallied for each section.

FIGURE 8.7 Tallying MLL Shadowing Marks

ACADEMIC SPEAKING (CHECK ONE)	ACADEMIC LISTENING ONE WAY OR TWO WAY (CHECK ONE)	STUDENT IS NOT LISTENING (CHECK ONE)	COMMENTS
☐ Student to student—1 ꤜꤜꤜꤜꤜ I	☐ One way or two way	☐ Reading or writing silently—1 ꤜꤜꤜꤜ ꤜꤜꤜꤜ ꤜꤜꤜꤜ II	
	☐ Student listening mostly to student—1 ꤜꤜꤜꤜ I		
☐ Student to teacher—2 IIII		☐ Student is off task—2 ꤜꤜꤜꤜ ꤜꤜꤜꤜ I	
	☐ Student listening mostly to teacher—2 ꤜꤜꤜꤜ ꤜꤜꤜꤜ ꤜꤜꤜꤜ II		
☐ Student to small group—3			
☐ Student to whole class—4	☐ Student listening mostly to small group—3		
☐ Teacher to student—5	☐ Student listening mostly to whole class—4		
☐ Teacher to small group—6			
☐ Teacher to whole class—7 ꤜꤜꤜꤜ ꤜꤜꤜꤜ ꤜꤜꤜꤜ III			

Figure 8.7 visually represents the sections of the MLL shadowing form that should be tallied by participants. Organizers of the training should create poster-sized versions of these four sections of the protocol, making them large enough so that participants can physically tally their responses using markers. Participants will then place their sticky note summaries in the last column, which should then be sorted by theme and patterns. Figure 8.8 is a picture of a completed MLL Shadowing Analysis Poster for a shadowing project.

FIGURE 8.8   MLL Shadowing Data Analysis Poster

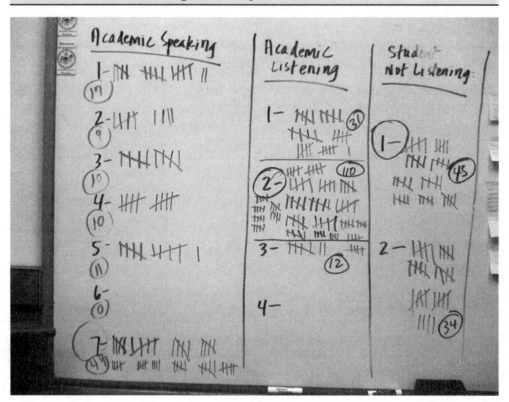

Once the tallies have been counted for each section, the most common mode under each section should be circled and shared with the group for further triangulation, with both the research literature and the achievement data provided for each student. This process further demonstrates to participants what may need to change instructionally for MLLs in order to change academic achievement systemically. The analysis also allows participants to see manifested in the room, with the tallies, that MLLs do indeed spend very little time speaking in the classroom setting. The statement is no longer esoteric in nature but becomes real and alive in the room. Physically seeing these tally marks quantifies the data and also allows participants to make decisions regarding what next steps should come after the MLL shadowing experience. In a virtual setting, tallies can be calculated using a Google doc that mirrors the poster above. This way, all participants can add their data at the same time, as well as analyze and discuss it. The following chapter will describe how to systemically leverage change from MLL shadowing.

REFERENCE

Gibbons, P. (2015). *Scaffolding language, scaffolding learning: Teaching second language learners in the mainstream classroom*. Portsmouth, NH: Heinemann.

CHAPTER 9

Using the Results to Leverage Change

Once the data have been analyzed and trends determined, a useful tool for determining teacher-level need is the Multilingual Learner (MLL) Shadowing Next Steps: Needs Assessment Form. Having been exposed to Think-Pair-Share, teacher-guided reporting, and productive group work on Days 1 and 2 of the MLL shadowing training, it is important for participating educators to determine where they feel most comfortable entering into professional development using these academic speaking strategies. These three strategies are also research-based ways to further engage all students and bring up the 2% of academic speaking that MLLs typically engage in. Once academic speaking has been amply developed, other components of academic language development—syntax, grammar, and vocabulary development—can also be incorporated into the classroom setting. This section will provide a process whereby the greatest areas of student need can be systemically focused on from the shadowing experience, with special attention to academic speaking and listening. It is important to remember, however, that because of the connections between speaking and writing, as well as listening and reading, educators are working on all aspects of academic language development when focusing on academic speaking.

Figure 9.1 can be used to determine next steps and focus areas from the 2-day MLL shadowing training. To begin, the first set of questions should be completed as a school team, and then the needs assessment (see Appendix A, page 140, or http://www.corwin.com/MLLshadowing) should be completed individually. This process allows school teams to begin thinking collectively about how to systemically address the needs of MLLs.

FIGURE 9.1   School Reflection Questions

School Reflection

- What urgency did this shadowing experience illuminate for you?
- Where in the ALD spectrum might students at your grade level benefit most?

  ○   Think-Pair-Share

  ○   teacher-guided reporting

  ○   productive group work

- What planning/next steps are needed?

The questions in Figure 9.1 are asked for the following reasons:

1. **What urgency did this shadowing experience illuminate for you?**
   This open-ended question allows participants to begin to consider that the sense of urgency from what was experienced must now become a plan in order for change to come about.

2. **Where in the academic language development (ALD) spectrum might students at your grade level benefit most?** This question will be used in conjunction with the needs assessment form, which asks participants to rank their level of comfort with each of the following academic language development strategies below (discussed in the next section):

   - Think-Pair-Share

   - teacher-guided reporting

   - productive group work

3. **What planning/next steps are needed?** This question allows participants to realize that their next steps must be explicitly laid out in order for them to take effect. A calendar planning form, the ALD Lesson Plan, can be found in Appendix B, page 155, and at http://www.corwin.com/MLLshadowing, for this purpose.

MLL Shadowing Next Steps: Needs Assessment

Using the MLL Shadowing Next Steps: Needs Assessment Form (see Appendix A, page 140, or http://www.corwin.com/MLLshadowing), educators are asked to rate their level of classroom need on a scale of 1 through 5 (1 being lowest and 5 being highest). This information, along with the student-level assessment results, should guide professional development efforts. Participants should fill this out individually and share results by school team, department, or grade level to find the most common area of need and entry point. This form can also be used by grade or department level to set goals and determine common next steps with academic oral language development. As teachers select strategies in common, they can begin to support each other, both in lesson design and in making adjustments to the ways in which strategies are utilized. The MLL Shadowing Next Steps: Needs Assessment Form is explained next and can be found in Appendix A, page 140, or at http://www.corwin.com/MLLshadowing.

Although the MLL shadowing results and assessment data analysis will allow needs to emerge very clearly, educators should be able to determine where their professional development efforts should begin. Otherwise, participants may feel overwhelmed by the level of need that has emerged from the MLL shadowing experience. Educators can begin by focusing on what they ranked as their highest level of need and, when they feel comfortable there, begin to embed other academic speaking strategies listed to their practice. It is important to note that systems—a school, district, or county office—should provide support and training in how to implement each of these strategies as a follow-up to MLL shadowing (information on how to do this can be found in the chapter that follows). Organizers of the training should embed and model these practices—Think-Pair-Share, teacher-guided reporting, and productive group work—into the initial MLL shadowing training itself. However, it is also essential to provide follow-up on how to implement each strategy in a classroom setting specifically, once the needs and focus areas have been determined from the MLL shadowing and data analysis itself. This will be described further in Chapter 10.

DISTRICT SHADOWING OPTIONS

Once educational systems have had their first MLL shadowing experience, they can choose to continue to shadow to monitor MLL progress in a variety of ways. Each of these options will be explained further in the section to come, along with entry points that a variety of districts have taken with MLL shadowing. Figure 9.2 lists some options for future MLL shadowing.

Additional MLL shadowing experiences can include, but are not limited to, the following options:

1. **Follow MLLs after providing schoolwide or districtwide personal development:** Once teachers have received follow-up training (see Chapter 10) on eliciting more oral academic language in the classroom using Think-Pair-Share and teacher-guided reporting, they can go into each other's classrooms looking for evidence of how MLLs in those classrooms are responding to and benefiting from the strategies. Additionally, teachers can examine MLL student work in order to determine next steps for instruction and strategy usage with this group of students. I use the tuning protocol with several of the schools I work with to analyze student work samples from the implementation of academic oral language development strategies.

FIGURE 9.2 Future Shadowing Experiences

> **Next Steps**
>
> - Future shadowing experiences:
>   - o Follow MLLs after providing schoolwide or districtwide personal development
>   - o Look for use of productive group work in classrooms
>   - o Follow MLLs at a variety of levels (elementary visit secondary and secondary visit elementary, or ELD levels)

2. **Look for use of productive group work in classrooms:** Once teachers have been trained in how to implement reciprocal teaching (in which students use the reading roles of summarizer, connector, questioner, and predictor to discuss a reading selection) or another group-work strategy, they may choose to go into each other's classrooms (by grade level or department) with the eight elements of productive group work (see Chapter 4) from Gibbons's (2015) work, to determine how those characteristics are assisting MLLs. Teachers can also plan next steps for instruction by determining which elements might need to be utilized more frequently.

3. **Follow MLLs at a variety of levels (elementary visit secondary and secondary visit elementary or by English language development [ELD] levels):** To determine how MLLs are progressing across a system, districts may have elementary schools visit secondary schools and vice versa to begin articulation across levels. This can also be done within feeder patterns or ELD levels; that is, elementary schools that feed into middle and high schools can shadow each other. Additionally, teachers who teach beginning-level ELD students can shadow MLLs at the end of the ELD spectrum in order to see their progression and needs.

All of these ideas for additional MLL shadowing options can assist with ensuring that the urgency apparent throughout the 2-day experience does not wane. In essence, MLL shadowing can be a way both to determine baseline needs and to monitor progress once specific MLL needs have been identified. As a seasoned teacher in Stanislaus County, California, has said, "I believe that MLL shadowing should be done each year so that we can monitor the progress of our MLLs and our programs" (Soto-Hinman, personal communication, 2006).

DISTRICT AND SCHOOL ENTRY POINTS

The Norwalk–La Mirada Unified School District in Norwalk, California, a district of 21,500 students and 23% MLLs, conducted a districtwide

MLL shadowing training, which began with administrators in the fall of 2010. As described in Chapter 6, all administrators, including district-office administrators, first attended half-day trainings on how to shadow an MLL. The actual MLL shadowing training at school sites followed this, with a debriefing session by elementary, middle, and high school participants, on 3 subsequent Fridays (Day 1 and 2 agendas can be found in Figures 9.3 and 9.4).

FIGURE 9.3 Day 1 Agenda of MLL Shadowing Training for Norwalk-La Mirada Unified

---

Norwalk–La Mirada Unified School District

MLL Shadowing

DAY 1 AGENDA

8:00—Registration and Continental Breakfast

8:30—Welcome and Agenda Review

8:40—Academic Speaking Review

10:00—Break

10:30—Active Listening Overview

12:00—Lunch

12:45—Shadowing Introduction/Practice With the Protocol

2:30—Day 2 Agenda Overview/Logistics/Student Profiles

3:00—Closing

PLEASE DON'T FORGET TO WEAR YOUR

DISTRICT ID TO THE OBSERVATION SCHOOL ON DAY 2.

Once the districtwide administrator training took place, several schools—one per level—volunteered to be model implementation sites for MLL shadowing with the district. This meant that a core group of teacher-leaders at each site decided to shadow MLLs and also to participate in the academic language development follow-up sessions with Dr. Soto as the facilitator. This group of teachers decided to work on the needs of MLLs. The district office and school site administrative teams decided to start with a small group of teachers at each school to create model classrooms and excitement around shadowing and meeting the needs of MLLs. At the high school level, six teachers from across the content areas met on five different dates to learn how to shadow, debrief the experience, and begin to embed academic language development strategies systemically into their instruction with MLLs. This small group of willing teachers, whose work leveraged additional buy-in, provided a powerful way to replicate the administrator MLL shadowing experience. Also, once teachers began using the ALD strategies, additional teachers were encouraged to observe these best practices in action and to shadow an MLL themselves. This process, then, becomes a significant way to leverage change from the MLL shadowing experience. First, starting with a small group of teachers and then adding the rest of the staff, word soon spread about the power of the shadowing experience. This process reminds educators that true systemic change is often grassroots and begins small. Teachers must feel that they have a voice in the change process and can choose entry points and strategies, especially at the beginning of the professional development sequence. The MLL Shadowing Next Steps: Needs Assessment can be used for that purpose and is included in Figure 9.5; in Appendix A, page 140; and at http://www.corwin .com/MLLshadowing.

FIGURE 9.4 Day 2 Agenda of MLL Shadowing Training for Norwalk-La Mirada Unified

---

Norwalk–La Mirada Unified School District

MLL Shadowing

DAY 2 AGENDA

School Site Visit Information

Johnston Elementary School

Premeeting Time: 7:45 AM

Los Alisos Middle School

Premeeting Time: 7:30 AM

John Glenn High School

Meeting Room: Library

Premeeting Time: 7:50 AM

8:00–10:00 AM—MLL Shadowing

10:00 AM—Break/Recess

10:15 AM—Shadowing Debriefing

11:15 AM—Wrap Up, Evaluations, PD Survey, Next Steps

Figure 9.5 describes the MLL shadowing follow-up regarding academic language development, which should be used with all teachers and administrators once they have shadowed an MLL.

FIGURE 9.5 MLL Shadowing Next Steps: Needs Assessment

On a scale of 1 through 5, with 1 being lowest and 5 being highest, which of the following areas do you consider to be the greatest need in your classroom?

1. Think-Pair-Share

         1   2   3   4   5

Comments:

_____

2. Teacher-Guided Reporting

Use of open-ended questions (requiring more than one-word responses)

         1   2   3   4   5

_____

Asking for linguistic clarification (grammar, specific language, etc.)

         1   2   3   4   5

Encouragement

         1   2   3   4   5

Recasting (restating student responses in academic language)

         1   2   3   4   5

Comments:

_____

3. Productive Group Work (e.g., Reciprocal Teaching, Socratic Seminar, Literature Circles, etc.)

         1   2   3   4   5

Comments:

_____

REFERENCE

Gibbons, P. (2015). *Scaffolding language, scaffolding learning: Teaching second language learners in the mainstream classroom*. Portsmouth, NH: Heinemann.

Next Steps With Shadowing Multilingual Learners

CHAPTER 10

Next Steps and Follow-Up to Shadowing Multilingual Learners

MLL FOLLOW-UP ON ACADEMIC LANGUAGE DEVELOPMENT

Multilingual learner (MLL) shadowing is the beginning of the learning and tailoring of needs for MLLs. MLL shadowing creates the awareness, but there must be a clear and focused plan to change practices for results to change for MLLs. Once next steps have been determined from the MLL shadowing experience, there must be ongoing professional development for teachers for MLLs to benefit from the changes in practices. This chapter will uncover three strategies that can be used to elicit more academic oral language development in the classroom setting.

THINK-PAIR-SHARE 2.0

Think-Pair-Share 2.0 is one of the best ways to begin to embed more academic speaking in a classroom setting. I like to call it Think-Pair-Share 2.0 because it is not your typical partner talk or even the typical Think-Pair-Share that you might be familiar with. Instead, Think-Pair-Share 2.0 creates accountability for talk on the part of the student, requires active listening, and ends with a consensus conversation to refine a pair's thinking. As mentioned in Chapter 4, August and Shanahan (2006) suggest that oral language development is the foundation of literacy. The academic oral language benefits for MLLs are expansive. Often, students are more comfortable presenting ideas to a larger group, especially when they have been able to practice with a supportive partner. Additionally, students' ideas, especially those of MLLs, become more refined through the three-step process embedded in Think-Pair-Share 2.0. If, according to August and Shanahan (2006) in the National Literacy Panel report, MLLs also benefit from more time and practice with content, the Think-Pair-Share process allows those ideas to become developed over time. When MLLs are sharing with a linguistic model (a student who is just above an MLL's ability but not one who will take over the conversation), the MLLs will benefit from hearing more language and higher levels of language, which they can then recycle in their own response. There can also be times, however, when higher-end students are grouped together so that they are also challenged.

If the benefits of academic speaking structures are expansive, then as educators, we must find ways and opportunities for students to talk in a linguistically rich environment. Pressley (1992) has suggested that students' learning is enhanced when they have many opportunities to elaborate on ideas through talk. In this way, students, especially MLLs, make meaning as they talk. The Think-Pair-Share 2.0 strategy, specifically, increases the kinds of personal communications necessary for students to internally process, organize, and retain ideas (Pimm, 1987). In order for this strategy to be effective, however, Think-Pair-Share 2.0 must be organized in order for it to be effective. Students, especially MLLs, should never be expected to effectively speak on topics until the strategy has been scaffolded for them. Some of the ways to scaffold the Think-Pair-Share 2.0 strategy include the use of metacognition via teacher think-alouds, ample modeling via fishbowls, and the scaffolding of each step in the process using specific techniques.

Metacognition via Think-Alouds

Metacognition is defined as thinking about one's thinking. One way to make one's thinking visible to students is via a think-aloud. This technique is especially helpful when modeling and beginning to incorporate Think-Pair-Share 2.0 in a classroom setting. Since each of the steps in Think-Pair-Share 2.0 should be scaffolded, one way to scaffold the thinking process is by unpacking one's thinking using the think-aloud strategy. A good way to begin this modeling is by using an open-ended and user-friendly question. For example, if *Grandfather's Journey* by Allen Say (1993), a book about a grandchild recalling his grandfather's immigration experience, had just been read, a question such as "What is your favorite part of the book?" may be used. Notice that this question is open-ended and does not have a right or wrong answer, so it allows for more language usage and modeling. Another scaffold can be the use of a reduced or simple text with an open-ended question so students can focus on the process of the Think-Pair-Share 2.0 and not have to focus on the content of the material.

The teacher will want to begin the modeling process by first being quiet and thinking about the question. Many students will want to call out the first thing on their mind when they are asked to think about a question. It is important to begin with the notion that we want students' best thoughts, and not their first thoughts, to emerge, so modeling that process will be paramount. When sharing the favorite part of the book, a teacher may model as shown in Figure 10.1, the Think-Pair-Share Summary.

FIGURE 10.1 Think-Pair-Share Summary

NONVERBAL CUES	VERBAL CUES
Think—Place your hand at your temple in order to demonstrate time to think about the question. As you think, try to focus on *the* most important ideas for clarity.	*There are so many parts of* Grandfather's Journey *that really resonate for me, so I really need to take some time and be silent about this in order to select the most important part for me.*
Pair—Turn toward your partner and make eye contact.	*I'm now ready to share with you the most important part of* Grandfather's Journey *for me.*
Share—Direct the conversation toward your partner and keep eye contact.	*I think the portion of the book that resonated most for me happens throughout the text, but especially at the end, when the grandchild begins to notice, and finally confirms, that his grandfather really felt that he never belonged anywhere—neither in Japan nor in the United States. The notion that immigrants seem to lose something of themselves, both in the place of origin and in the new country, is something that I connect to because of my mother's experience as an immigrant in the United States.*

Notice that this classroom scenario breaks down each of the specific Think-Pair-Share 2.0 moves for the student. First, the teacher takes some silent time in order to collect her thoughts; only then does she make direct eye contact and share only key ideas that resonate for her from *Grandfather's Journey*. Once the teacher has modeled the thinking process with this strategy, she may bring another student up to the front of the room to further model how to complete Think-Pair-Share 2.0 before releasing all of the responsibility to the students with the strategy. Figure 10.2 shows the scaffolded steps for Think-Pair-Share 2.0.

FIGURE 10.2 Scaffolded Steps for Think-Pair-Share

1. **Think:** Students think independently about the question that has been posed, forming ideas of their own.
2. **Pair:** Students are grouped in pairs to discuss their thoughts. Using a sentence frame, this step allows students to articulate their ideas and to consider those of others.
3. **Share:** Student pairs share their ideas with a larger group, such as the whole class.

   ○ Often, students are more comfortable presenting ideas to a group with the support of a partner.

   ○ In addition, students' ideas have become more refined through this three-step process.

SOURCE: Adapted from Soto-Hinman and Hetzel (2009).

Additionally, note that it is the unpacking of each step in the process, including the nonverbals that are associated with them, that will allow a student to be successful with this strategy. Putting one's finger at the temple becomes a nonverbal cue for the importance of really giving one time to be silent and think through responses instead of just saying whatever is on one's mind. Facing one's partner and making eye contact scaffolds the appropriate nonverbal cues needed when having an academic discussion with a colleague. Finally, the first two steps in conjunction with the nonverbal cues allow one to respond fully and coherently and to make one's thoughts clear to another person. Each of these steps allows students to better comprehend, apply, and internalize information at a level that they wouldn't be able to do without such scaffolding of thought.

Think-Pair-Share Adaptation for Primary Grades

In the primary elementary school grades, Think-Pair-Share 2.0 cards can be used so that students can remember when to use each of the steps. One card should have a mouth and *speaking* on it; the other card should have an ear and *listening* on it. These cards can be laminated so that they are not easily damaged. Students should hold the appropriate card when they are either listening or speaking. When a student is speaking, he or she should hold the card with the mouth on it (photocopied in green, to go and speak), and when a student is listening (photocopied in red, to stop and listen), he or she should hold the card with an ear on it. Figure 10.3 demonstrates the additional visual reminder that the speaking and listening cards create for primary students to follow each of the Think-Pair-Share steps.

FIGURE 10.3 Additional Visual Reminders for Speaking and Listening

Note to Teacher: Print this in red (to stop and listen)

Listening

(remember to Look, Lean, and Listen)

"What my partner said was . . ."

"What I'm hearing you say is . . ."

Note to Teacher: Print this in green (to go and speak)

Speaking

(remember to think and share your best thinking with your partner)

"I think/believe that . . ."

"In my opinion . . ."

IMAGE SOURCES: pixabay.com/OpenClipart-and pixabay.com/LMpolepy

Think-Pair-Share Graphic Organizer

Another scaffold that can be used includes the graphic organizer shown in Figure 10.4. This becomes yet another strategy that will keep students accountable for both speaking and listening once modeling via metacognition has been used. The graphic organizer can also be used in conjunction with metacognitive modeling, especially when students need a tangible guide for each of the steps. It is important to note that explicit modeling of how to use the graphic organizer will be needed. The following are some ideas about how to do that.

FIGURE 10.4   DOK Question Stems

DOK 1

- Can you recall _____?
- When did _____ happen?
- Who was _____?
- How can you recognize _____?
- What is _____?
- How can you find the meaning of _____?
- Can you recall _____?
- Can you select _____?
- How would you write _____?
- What might you include on a list about _____?
- Who discovered _____?
- What is the formula for _____?
- Can you identify _____?
- How would you describe _____?

DOK 2

- Can you explain how _____ affected _____?
- How would you apply what you learned to develop _____?
- How would you compare _____?
- Contrast _____?
- How would you classify _____?
- How are _____ alike? Different?
- How would you classify the type of _____?
- What can you say about _____?
- How would you summarize _____?
- How would you summarize _____?
- What steps are needed to edit _____?
- When would you use an outline to _____?
- How would you estimate _____?
- How could you organize _____?
- What would you use to classify _____?
- What do you notice about _____?

DOK 3

- How is _____ related to _____?
- What conclusions can you draw _____?
- How would you adapt _____ to create a different _____?
- How would you test _____?
- Can you predict the outcome if _____?
- What is the best answer? Why?
- What conclusion can be drawn from these three texts?
- What is your interpretation of this text?
- Support your rationale.
- How would you describe the sequence of _____?
- What facts would you select to support _____?
- Can you elaborate on the reason _____?
- What would happen if _____?
- Can you formulate a theory for _____?
- How would you test _____?
- Can you elaborate on the reason _____?

DOK 4

- Write a thesis, drawing conclusions from multiple sources.
- Design and conduct an experiment. Gather information to develop alternative explanations for the results of an experiment.
- Write a research paper on a topic.
- Apply information from one text to another text to develop a persuasive argument.
- What information can you gather to support your idea about _____?
- DOK 4 would most likely be the writing of a research paper or applying information from one text to another text to develop a persuasive argument.
- DOK 4 requires time for extended thinking.

SOURCE: Developed by Dr. Norman Webb and Flip Chart developed by Myra Collins. Reprinted with permission.

Question/Prompt Section

Notice that the first column includes an area to determine the questions or prompts that teachers would like students to think through. It is important for teachers to think through these questions or prompts carefully ahead of time so that the questions themselves require and allow for extensive talk. Such questions and prompts should occur carefully in the planning stage and can be developed with colleagues by either grade level or department level. Questions and prompts should also ultimately connect back to the standards, content, or comprehension strategies being taught as well as the objective of the lesson itself. Questions should not be formulated randomly in the middle of teaching. Teachers may choose to compose questions through collaborating during lesson-planning time.

Teachers should focus on formulating questions at depth of knowledge (DOK) levels 3 and 4 for Think-Pair-Share 2.0, while DOK levels 1 and 2 can be utilized for partner talks. Students can also be taught to use these resources in order to formulate questions when reciprocal teaching is introduced. Figure 10.4 includes question stems at DOK levels 1 through 4.

Thinking Section

The second column is a section where students can write down what they are thinking about before they discuss it with their partners. Using this portion of the graphic organizer before having students share allows students to become clearer about their ideas. In essence, it requires students to do the thinking they'll need before they speak. Remember that even students with a lot of language, like gifted students, need time to refine their thinking. These students usually say the first thing on their mind, and instead, we want them to give us their best thoughts. It is important to remember, however, that MLLs at lower levels of English language development may be able to produce more oral rather than written language. If this is the case, providing a close passage or language frame, along with a word wall for key vocabulary (if needed), may be appropriate. For example, "My idea was ...," or "My partner's idea was ...," and "Together we thought...." Providing students with the language allows them to focus their attention on the content. It is also important to model how to use each type of language frame so that students understand how to use them. Lastly, teachers should vary language frames according to the purpose of the conversation. The same language frames should be used all year long. See language frames in Figure 10.5 and in Appendix B.

Listening Section

The third column requires accountability for the sharing and listening processes. Once students have had time to think through the question or prompt and when they share their ideas with each other, they are then required to listen actively in order to summarize their partners' ideas. Only after students listen actively should they be allowed to summarize. It is important to remind students that active listening and/or paraphrasing is connected to the ability to summarize when reading.

FIGURE 10.5 Language Strategies for Active Classroom Participation

DISCOURSE SENTENCE FRAMES FOR MULTIPLE PURPOSES		
	Express an Opinion I believe that _____ will happen because _____. I like the story because _____. My answer is _____ because _____.	**Predict** I can predict that _____ because _____. I predict _____. The prediction is based on _____.
	Ask for Clarification Can you explain what you mean? I was wondering _____ when _____.	**Paraphrase** I am understanding you to say _____ because _____. What I'm hearing from you is _____. Is that correct?
	Summarization The passage is mostly about _____ because _____. Some important details are _____ and _____.	**Acknowledge Ideas** I agree with my colleague because _____. I want to build upon my colleague's ideas _____.
	Report a Partner's Idea My colleague suggested that _____. _____ pointed out that _____.	**Report a Group's Idea** We came to consensus on _____. We mostly agreed, but here's where we didn't _____.
	Disagree I have to kindly disagree because _____. I had a different way of looking at this because _____.	**Offer a Suggestion** I wonder if _____. That was a good start, but how about _____.
	Affirm I appreciate your thinking because _____. Thank you for your helping me to understand _____.	**Hold the Floor** As I was suggesting _____. Let me think about that and get back to you.

SOURCE: Adapted from Kate Kinsella and Dutro (2010).

The listening section of the graphic organizer becomes a place for students to record and organize their own ideas. But it also requires careful listening and an accounting of their partners' responses. Remind students that they should not merely swap papers for this section. An example of this type of additional scaffold is "The most important part of the text is _____ because _____." Or "I completed the math problem by _____ because _____." Notice that with the addition of the *because* section of the language stem, students are required to provide more language and thinking regarding why they responded as they did.

Consensus/Commonalities Section

The final step that educators may choose to eventually incorporate with Think-Pair-Share 2.0 is coming to consensus around ideas. There are four options for the consensus section of the organizer, as follows:

- **What I said and justify why**—As a pair, there is consensus to share what partner #1 has said. Each pair should justify why they made this selection.

- **What my partner said and justify why**—As a pair, there is consensus to share what partner #2 has said. Each pair should justify why they made this selection.

- **A combination and justify why**—As a pair, there is consensus to share a combination of what was discussed because there were similarities. If commonalities are not present, then students should try to put their two ideas together ("I said . . . and my partner said . . ."). Each pair should justify why they made this selection.

- **A whole new idea and justify why**—As a pair, oftentimes as a result of the conversation, students come up with new ideas and/or perhaps new solutions. Each pair should justify why they made this selection.

This section is meant to expand one's own ways of thinking and to further clarify and provide precise thinking. Since meaning is socially constructed, students' responses should influence each other via the pairing segment of Think-Pair-Share 2.0. In the end, students should have grown, evolved, and been provided with a broader perspective on an issue or question due to the sharing experience.

Fishbowl of Think-Pair-Share With Graphic Organizer

Using the Think-Pair-Share 2.0 organizer in Figure 10.7, the teacher can model each of these steps in a fishbowl setting by asking a student who is effective at Think-Pair-Share to model the process with the rest of the class as all students look on. The teacher can work with a student in advance of the fishbowl in order to prepare them for the academic conversation. The benefit of this becomes the gradual release of responsibility for independent practice in pairs. This gives students yet one more model of how to complete a strategy that may be new to them. Some students may not understand how to effectively use the strategy until they see it modeled with another student, even though the teacher has been explicit with the think-aloud. The more scaffolding that is done up front with students, the more successful they will be when they are expected to pair-share on their own.

FIGURE 10.6 Scaffolding Think-Pair-Share 2.0

OPEN-ENDED QUESTION OR PROMPT	WHAT I THOUGHT (SPEAKING)	WHAT MY PARTNER THOUGHT (LISTENING)	WHAT WE WILL SHARE (CONSENSUS)
Academic language stems for speaking: *"What I thought was . . . because . . ."* Academic language stem for listening: *"What my partner thought was . . . because . . ."* Academic language stem for consensus: *"What we thought was . . . because . . ."*			

SOURCE: Created by author, based on Lyman (1981).

Using the Power Walk for Accountable Talk

Even with the levels of Think-Pair-Share scaffolding suggested in this section, it is essential for teachers to monitor the conversations by walking around the room. This is called the Power Walk (Soto-Hinman & Hetzel, 2009), whereby the teacher holds students accountable for appropriate academic speaking but also listens in for important ideas that can be shared with the entire group. The final step of having students share important ideas with the entire group also provides message redundancy and abundancy. Those ideas that students did not understand through their own thinking or by listening to their partner can finally become clearer with a third level of language practice, in which they hear the explanation or thinking of another person whose response resonates for them. This layering of language and content provides the kind of oral language and academic support that MLLs need.

Once teachers become comfortable with Think-Pair-Share 2.0, it is helpful to have them try on additional strategies that address the essential components of academic English. According to linguists and scholars, the essential components of academic English are academic vocabulary, syntax, grammar, and the register of language. Think-Pair-Share 2.0 addresses the register of language—that is, knowing the difference between academic and social language, as well as in what context to use each. The following section will address how to explicitly teach academic vocabulary with MLLs.

FRAYER MODEL

The Frayer model is an explicit way to teach academic vocabulary to MLLs. The four steps to the Frayer model include: (1) determining examples and characteristics associated with the target word; (2) determining nonexamples associated with the target word, which includes words and concepts closely

---

FIGURE 10.7 Frayer Model Graphic Organizer

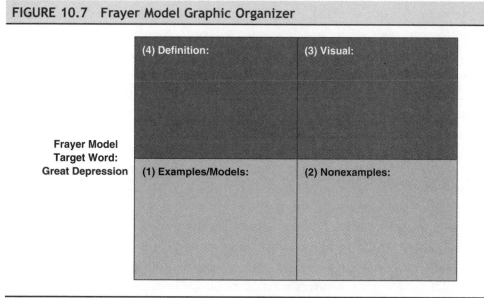

associated with the target word but not quite it; (3) a visual association that connects to the linguistic label for the word; and (4) a student's own definition of the target word. The power of the Frayer model is in students eventually developing their own definition, which they are more likely to retain and recall than a dictionary definition. The additional steps of determining examples and nonexamples, as well as a visual, will provide additional scaffolding and support for the target word and definition. Figure 10.9 is the graphic organizer used for the Frayer model. Notice that the steps are counterclockwise. This is intentional, as the strategy was not initially created for MLLs, but the steps have been reordered so that they do support MLLs.

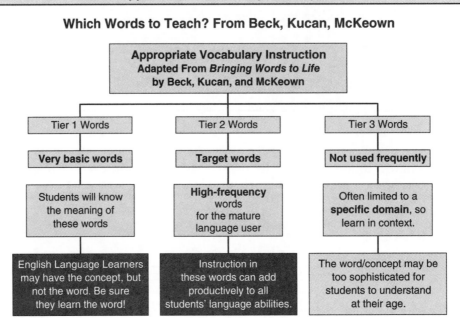

FIGURE 10.8 Tiered Approach to Vocabulary Development

Which Words to Teach? From Beck, Kucan, McKeown

The Frayer model strategy (1969) works best with Tier 2 and 3 words (Beck, McKeown, & Kucan, 2013). Tier 2 words are high-frequency words, such as *analyze* or *summarize*, which go across content areas. Tier 3 words are discipline-specific words that are discipline or content-area specific, such as *the Great Depression* in history/social science or *zero pairs* in math. Teachers should select three to five Tier 2 and/or 3 words, which are thematic or larger concept words for the Frayer model. Figure 10.8 unpacks the tiered vocabulary approach by Beck, McKeown, and Kucan (2013).

After three to five Tier 2 and 3 words have been selected for a unit, it is essential to build background knowledge around each word, so that MLLs are able to come up with examples and nonexamples of the target word, and eventually their own definition. Fisher and Frey (2010) suggest that there are direct and indirect ways to build background knowledge. Some direct ways include lab experiments, field trips, hands-on activities, guest speakers, simulations, and/or the use of tiles or manipulatives in math. Indirect ways to build background knowledge include

FIGURE 10.9 Completed Frayer Model Organizer

(4) Definition:	(3) Visual:
The coronavirus is ____, ____, and ____ because _____.	

	(1) Examples/Characteristics:	(2) Nonexamples:
Frayer Model Target Word: Coronavirus	• Tough bug to kick • Wash hands • Keeps you at home • Easily spread • Must socially distance • A kind of virus • Germs so small you can't see them • Float in the air via tiny drops of water • Catch COVID-19 illness	• Seasonal flu • Easier bug to kick • Keeps us at home for less time • Somewhat contagious

IMAGE SOURCE: pixabay.com/qimono

pre-planned web searches, using a series of photos, viewing short video clips, or reading selections on a topic. Once MLLs have adequately built background knowledge around a word, they can then successfully complete each step in the graphic organizer as shown in Figure 10.10. Before students completed the graphic organizer on page 124, they watched a video about the coronavirus and read the book *Coronavirus: A Book for Children* by Jenner, Wilson, and Roberts (2020). Notice that students have come up with ample examples and non-examples. They can now use the examples to assist them to developing their own definition using the sentence frame.

QIMONOA PRODUCTIVE GROUP-WORK MODEL: RECIPROCAL TEACHING

Reciprocal teaching is a manageable way to enter into productive group work because it can be used across grade levels and content areas. Additionally, since there are four roles associated with reciprocal teaching, this is an effective way to train students to work in groups and keep them accountable for the work. The four roles that are used with reciprocal teaching are as follows:

1. Summarizer—The student determines the three most important ideas from a selection.

2. Questioner—Three questions are posed from the selection.

3. Connector—The student makes a text-to-text, text-to-world, and text-to-life connection from the selection read.

4. Predictor—The student predicts what might happen next or what might be different if the main ideas within a text were used.

FIGURE 10.10 Reciprocal Teaching as Productive Group Work

Summarizer	Connector
*Identify what you think are the **three most important events/details from the reading and explain why they are important and how they are connected**.*	*Make **at least three connections** between ideas or events in the reading to **your own experience, the world around you, or other texts**.*
Questioner	**Predictor**
*Pose **at least three questions about the reading**; these could include questions that **address confusing parts** of the reading or thought **questions** that the reading makes you wonder about.*	*Identify **at least three text-related predictions**; these predictions should be based on new developments in the reading, and your predictions should help the group to **anticipate what will happen next**.*
Summarizer	**Connector**
In your own words, identify the three most important ideas from the text and justify why they are the most important.	*Good readers make connections as they read. Make three types of connections to the text that you just read: (1) text to text; (2) text to life; (3) text to world.*
Questioner	**Predictor**
Good readers also ask themselves questions as they read. Think of three questions that you had as you read, including something that you wondered about or perhaps something that was confusing.	*Make three text-supported predictions. A text-supported prediction means that you are predicting something that can be justified by evidence from the text that you just read.*

SOURCE: Westerhold and Kagan (1998).

Figure 10.11 summarizes each of the reciprocal teaching roles, which must be taught explicitly to students. It is essential that the teacher model the correct and complete usage of each role so that students can be successful with each strategy once they are expected to complete their roles in groups or independently. Many times teachers become frustrated with group work because students are off task or do not know how to complete the work expected of them. In this way, the gradual release of responsibility to independent practice is essential to success with reciprocal teaching. The teacher should begin the modeling of reciprocal teaching with a simple text or a selection that the class has read before. Beginning in this way allows students to focus on the strategy and not become discouraged by the difficulty of the text. Once students are familiar with the text selection, the teacher should model the analysis of the text using one strategy at a time, perhaps one strategy per day, so that students are clear about the differences. Please also note that the language frames for each reciprocal teaching role (also included in the appendix) provides students with the language by which to begin their academic conversation. For example, as the teacher reads *Stellaluna* (Cannon, 1993)—a story about a bird that becomes separated from her mother, lives with a bat community for a time, and learns about adapting and acclimating to differences—she can also model reading the text from each of the reciprocal teaching role perspectives.

If students had just engaged in an instructional read-aloud modeled by the teacher, she can also model a think-aloud with the class in order to determine the most important portions of *Stellaluna*. The teacher may begin this process by having students work in pairs to Think-Pair-Share with a partner about the most important ideas. Those ideas can then be clustered on a web, and then the class can prioritize what the most important ideas actually were. Some of those important ideas may include the specific differences between bats and birds or the importance of being accepting of those differences. Once the class has collaboratively sifted through and come to consensus regarding the most important ideas, they can be added to the summarizer portion of the graphic organizer.

Similarly, the teacher can model asking higher-order questions for the questioner role. With *Stellaluna*, the teacher can model how to structure effective questions.

- What was the author's intent with the text?

- What can we learn from Stellaluna's experience with the bats?

- How does this story apply to your own life?

With the predictor role, students can consider what might have happened if Stellaluna had never been separated from her mom. Additional predictions might include what the birds might have done had they never met Stellaluna and what Stellaluna's mother felt like when she was reunited with her child. Using a think-aloud scaffold, the teacher can model formulating effective predictions that advance comprehension and understanding of the text. This strategy can assist with not having predictions that are random and unfocused.

With the connector role, students can connect *Stellaluna* to another text they have read regarding being accepting of differences. For example, *Stellaluna* can be connected to a text on Dr. Martin Luther King. Students can also connect how they personally might or might not have been accepted by others. Finally, students can connect to a situation in the world in which someone was not accepted due to their differences, such as during segregation.

Only after the reciprocal teaching strategy has been thoroughly and effectively scaffolded with an entire class should students be expected to accurately and effectively complete each role on their own in groups. Once this modeling has been done, teachers can count students off one through four and assign each student one of the roles. Each group of four will become a home group, in which students will later share their specific roles. All of the same number groups will become the expert group, in which students can congregate together to complete their role and come to consensus regarding their responses. The expert step, in which students are grouped by like roles, provides an additional language and content scaffold so students can effectively share their specific roles with their home group.

Once students have completed and come to consensus about their specific roles within their expert group, they are now ready to share with their home group. It is important to note that this process places every student, including MLLs, in a significant mastery role. Additionally, MLLs have been given the opportunity to practice oral language twice—by contributing to the expert group and by sharing with their home group. The accountability component of having each person with a specific role requires each student to contribute to the rest of the group, because those students are needed for everyone to be successful with the material. The teacher can then have select representatives share each of the four roles with the whole class. This not only allows students to hear the material one more time but also allows them to hear the same message several times and in several different ways.

It is also important to note that the teacher should be walking around the room, listening in on conversations, keeping students accountable to appropriate levels of talk, and selecting the students who will share with the entire group. Only when this level of modeling of productive group work is provided, in which students move from whole-group into independent practice, will students truly experience effective and productive group work. Although the process may appear intensive at the outset, the training is worthwhile, as students will become skilled at in-depth conversations, which will be valuable with both language acquisition and comprehension of content.

RECIPROCAL TEACHING ACROSS THE CONTENT AREAS

Reciprocal teaching also lends itself to expository or informational texts across the content areas. The following lesson was developed for the Santa Clara County Office of Education Professional Development Consortium for Teachers of English Learners. The lesson is a ninth-grade biology lesson on DNA. The goal of the lesson is to help MLLs transfer reciprocal teaching to other content areas, as well as to internalize and comprehend difficult concepts in biology. It is important to note that before students engaged in reciprocal teaching, a brief lecture on DNA, using visuals, was provided by the teacher. The following is a brief lesson plan of the key components of the lesson.

- **Content objective for this lesson:** This lesson is designed to help students recall and comprehend key information regarding DNA in expository text.

- **Identify academic language outcome:** This lesson will integrate listening, speaking, reading, and writing modes to help students use academic English in science.

- **Identify English learner challenges:** English learners, especially at the intermediate or middle levels and beyond, struggle with expository text. They struggle with using academic English in the content areas to describe key concepts.

- **State language objective:** The target audience for this lesson is early advanced/advanced-level ELD students (Levels 4 and 5).

The specifics of using the reciprocal teaching strategy for this lesson are explained in Figure 10.11.

FIGURE 10.11 Reciprocal Teaching for Ninth-Grade Biology

Summarizer	Connector
In your own words, summarize three key ideas about DNA replication.	Make a text-to-text, text-to-world, or text-to-life connection to DNA replication. (For example, students might want to make a text-to-world connection between DNA replication and cloning.)
Questioner	**Predictor**
Write down three questions that you still have about DNA replication.	Write down three predictions that you have about what would happen if proofreading were not done during replication.

SOURCE: Adapted from Soto-Hinman and Hetzel (2009).

For this lesson, students worked in groups of four using the reciprocal teaching roles—summarizer, connector, questioner, and predictor. Each student completed the following, according to each role:

- **Summarizer**—In your own words, summarize three key ideas about DNA replication.

- **Connector**—Make a text-to-text, text-to-world, or text-to-life connection to DNA replication. (Hint: You might want to make a text-to-world connection between DNA replication and cloning.)

- **Questioner**—Write down three questions that you still have about DNA replication.

- **Predictor**—Write down three predictions you have about what would happen if proofreading were done during replication.

Once students had completed their reciprocal teaching roles using the template distributed, they also participated in group conversations discussing the material. Students used their reciprocal teaching role cards (see Appendix B, page 152) to engage in a conversation about their assigned role so that they also practiced specific language for scientific discourse. For example, the summarizer began his portion of the conversation by saying, "The three most important things I learned about DNA replication were...." Using reciprocal teaching across the content areas ensures that rigorous academic content and language are internalized and comprehended.

The Tuning Protocol: Reflection and Accountability for Strategy Usage

Once teachers have begun implementing one or all of the three academic language development strategies—Think-Pair-Share, reciprocal teaching, and teacher-guided reporting—they can begin reflecting on how well the strategies have been received by MLLs by analyzing student work samples using the tuning protocol. It is the power of instructional conversations, with a focus on what the student work is telling educators, that allows for reflective teaching and promotes collaboration. According to Blythe, Allen, and Powell (1999),

> The tuning protocol was originally developed as a means for the five high schools in the Coalition of Essential School's Exhibitions Project to receive feedback and fine-tune their developing student assessment systems, including exhibitions, portfolios and design projects. . . . Since its trial run in 1992, the tuning protocol has been widely used and adapted for professional development purposes in and among schools across the country. (p. 1)

Specifically, the power is in the fact that educators get to determine the focus question regarding the analysis of the student work. That is, the educator sets the lens for how the student work should be analyzed, but the student work itself also tells the story of what needs to be done next in terms of instruction. The reflective conversations had by educators around the student work samples being analyzed allow everyone in the room to benefit regarding how slight alterations in the strategy usage can create the most benefit for MLLs. Additionally, the best practices can be shared by other educators who have used the strategy in a more effective way. Using the same cycle to analyze student work over time allows educators to sustain a focus on strategy usage and implementation so that they are well supported as they try new instructional practices. There are five main steps to the tuning protocol, which are explained in Figure 10.12. Please also note that the tuning protocol has been included in Appendix B (page 156), and at http://www.corwin.com/MLLshadowing, for use in a professional development or collaboration session.

FIGURE 10.12 The Tuning Protocol

The tuning protocol is a process for looking at a piece of curriculum and receiving feedback to incorporate into future planning.

Presentation: (5 minutes)

To begin, the presenter explains his or her work while other participants are silent.

The presenter should speak to

1. Assignment or prompt that generated the student work
2. Student learning goals for the work
3. Samples of the work
4. Evaluation format (scores, rubric, test)
5. Differentiation for different MLLs and skills levels

And then . . .

6. Ask a focusing question for feedback (Example: How can I differentiate the project? What are some interim activities? How can I teach writing skills?)

Examination of Curriculum: (5 minutes)

Silent Examination of Paperwork Provided

Participants look at presented curriculum and take notes on where it seems to be in tune with goals and where there might be problems. Make note of warm (positive) and cool (constructive next steps around focus question only) feedback and probing questions.

Clarifying Questions: (5 minutes)

Group members can ask clarifying questions of the presenter that have brief, factual answers. (Example: How many days is the project?)

Warm and Cool Feedback: (15 minutes)

Each participant shares feedback with the presenter, who is silent and taking notes. Participants identify where the work seems to meet with goals and then continue with possible disconnects and problems. They provide suggestions. Make sure to address the focus question.

Reflection: (5 minutes)

Presenter speaks to those comments and questions that he or she chooses while participants are silent. This is not a good time to defend oneself but a time to explore interesting ideas that came out of the feedback session.

Implementation of the Tuning Protocol With Schools

I have used the tuning protocol with teachers, alongside the academic language development strategies outline, in both the Norwalk–La Mirada Unified School District in Norwalk, California, and the Lucia Mar Unified School District in Arroyo Grande, California. From January through June 2011, I worked with teacher-leaders from various grade levels and content areas at Los Alisos Middle School and John Glenn High School in Norwalk–La Mirada Unified School District, as well as at Dorothea Lange Elementary School in Lucia Mar Unified School District. All three schools used Think-Pair-Share in their classrooms over the 6-month period and analyzed student work samples from a variety of grade levels and departments, using the following cycle:

January: Introduction to Think-Pair-Share/Grade Level or Content-Area Planning for Think-Pair-Share

February: Analyzing MLL Work Samples From Think-Pair-Share/Next Steps With Think-Pair-Share

March: Creating Open-Ended Questions/Analyzing Student Work Samples From Think-Pair-Share

April: Analyzing Student Work Samples From Think-Pair-Share/ Classroom Observations of Think-Pair-Share

May: Next Steps on Creating Consensus for Think-Pair-Share/Analyzing Student Work Samples From Think-Pair-Share/Classroom Observations of Think-Pair-Share

June: Analyzing Student Work Samples From Think-Pair-Share/ Classroom Observations of Think-Pair-Share/Next Steps for Next School Year

Notice that the cycle of inquiry each time included the analysis of student work samples from Think-Pair-Share. As teachers became comfortable with using the strategy itself, they also worked on becoming reflective about their practice using the tuning protocol. Throughout the 6 months, teachers became better at analyzing student work from linguistic and not merely content standpoints. Since the student work analyzed was mostly MLL samples, it was important to determine the students' academic language needs and not merely their content development. The ongoing analysis of student work in teacher teams provided support, accountability for strategy usage, and constant reflection over time. Since the National Staff Development Council (August & Shanahan, 2006) tells us that teachers need close to 50 hours of professional development to improve their skills and their students' learning, the tuning protocol, alongside implementation of Think-Pair-Share over time, allowed teachers to become really good at using one academic oral language development strategy before moving on to another strategy (which was the plan for fall 2011). Again, it is not about how many strategies are being implemented but ensuring that those that are being used are implemented well. We do not need 50 different strategies in schools but a few strategies that are used well and directly support and benefit MLLs in content and language.

Conclusion

The three strategies addressed—Think-Pair-Share 2.0, Frayer model, and reciprocal teaching—are research-based, strategy entry points that can elicit more academic language development for MLLs in the classroom setting. These strategies also ensure that the MLL shadowing experience is leveraged into immediate next steps to systemically change practice and achievement for MLLs. These strategies are not the only ones that can be implemented to effect change, but they are the ones that have been used by the author with several schools and districts in order to begin to change academic oral language development practices for MLLs. Only by implementing such strategies and being reflective about our teaching practices can we begin to find the language in the curriculum again, elicit the voices of MLLs in our classrooms, and begin to systemically change instruction and achievement for this group of students. As you implement each strategy, remember the difference that these strategies would have made for the MLL that you shadowed, as well as the difference that you *will* make for all of the MLLs in your classroom. Remember your Josue.

REFERENCES

August, D., & Shanahan, T. (2006). *Developing literacy in second language learners: Report of the national literacy panel on language minority children and youth*. Mahwah, NJ: Erlbaum.

Beck, I., McKeown, M., & Kucan, L. (2013). *Bringing words to life: Robust vocabulary instruction*. New York: Guilford Press.

Blythe, T., Allen, D., & Powell, B. (1999). *Looking together at student work*. New York: Teachers College Press.

Cannon, J. (1993). *Stellaluna*. New York: Harcourt.

Collins, M., & Webb, N. (2006). *Depth of knowledge flip book*. Kirksville, MO: Northeast Regional Professional Development.

Fisher, D., & Frey, N. (2010). *Building and activating background knowledge*. Reston, VA: Principal Leadership.

Frayer, D., Frederick, W. C., & Klausmeier, H. J. (1969). *A schema for testing the level of cognitive mastery*. Madison: Wisconsin Center for Education Research.

Jenner, E., Wilson, K., & Roberts, N. (2020). *Coronavirus: A book for children*. London, England: Nosy Crow.

Kinsella, K., & Feldman, L. (2006). *Language strategies for active classroom participation*. Author.

Lyman, F. (1981). The responsive classroom discussion: The inclusion of all students. *Mainstreaming Digest*. College Park, MD, University of Maryland.

Pimm, D. (1987). *Speaking mathematically: Communication in mathematics classrooms*. London, England: Routledge.

Pressley, M. (1992). Beyond direct explanation: Transactional instruction of reading comprehension strategies. *Elementary School Journal, 92*, 513–555.

Say, A. (1993). *Grandfather's journey*. New York: Houghton Mifflin.

Soto-Hinman, I., & Hetzel, J. (2009). *The literacy gaps: Building bridges for English language learners and Standard English learners*. Thousand Oaks, CA: Corwin.

Wiederhold, C. W., & Kagan, S. (1998). *Cooperative learning and higher level thinking: The Q matrix*. San Clemente, CA: Kagan Cooperative.

Appendix A

Shadowing Multilingual Learners Resources

Road to Reclassification: Academic Goal Setting

My Name is: _____

My Grade is: _____ My ID number: _____

Years in the United States: _____ ELD Teacher: _____

CURRENT GRADES	1ST SEMESTER (LAST SCHOOL YR)	2ND SEMESTER (LAST SCHOOL YR)
Math: _____	Math: _____	Math: _____
Science: _____	Science: _____	Science: _____
History: _____	History: _____	History: _____
English: _____	English: _____	English: _____
Elective/PE: _____	Elective/PE: _____	Elective/PE: _____
Elective: _____	Elective: _____	Elective: _____

CURRENT GRADES	3RD SEMESTER (LAST SCHOOL YR)	4TH SEMESTER (LAST SCHOOL YR)
Math: _____	Math: _____	Math: _____
Science: _____	Science: _____	Science: _____
History: _____	History: _____	History: _____
English: _____	English: _____	English: _____
Elective/PE: _____	Elective/PE: _____	Elective/PE: _____
Elective: _____	Elective: _____	Elective: _____

My greatest strength is: _____

My area of need is: _____

What am I learning about myself as a multilingual learner?

WHAT RESOURCES ARE YOU TAKING ADVANTAGE OF?

- ☐ Attending after-school tutoring/homework help

- ☐ Monitoring grades on Ayres (data system)

- ☐ Communicating with teacher(s)

- ☐ Setting a homework routine

- ☐ Using an agenda

GOAL SETTING

First Semester:

What is the one area you want to work on? _____

_____

_____

What steps can you take to help you succeed in that area?

- ☐ _____

- ☐ _____

- ☐ _____

What is one thing that your parent can do to support you?

- ☐ _____

What is one thing that your teacher can do to support you?

- ☐ _____

_____

MLL Shadowing Protocol Form

Student: _____ School: _____ ELD Level: _____

Gender: _____ Grade Level: _____ Years in U.S. Schools: _____ Years in District: _____

TIME	SPECIFIC STUDENT ACTIVITY/ LOCATION OF STUDENT FIVE-MINUTE INTERVALS	ACADEMIC SPEAKING (CHECK ONE)	ACADEMIC LISTENING ONE WAY OR TWO WAY (CHECK ONE)	STUDENT IS NOT LISTENING (CHECK ONE)	COMMENTS
		☐ Student to student—**1** ☐ Student to teacher—**2** ☐ Student to small group—**3** ☐ Student to whole class—**4** ☐ Teacher to student—**5** ☐ Teacher to small group—**6** ☐ Teacher to whole class—**7**	**One way or two way** ☐ Student listening mostly to student—**1** ☐ Student listening mostly to teacher—**2** ☐ Student listening mostly to small group—**3** ☐ Student listening mostly to whole class—**4**	☐ Reading or writing silently—**1** ☐ Student is off task—**2**	
		☐ Student to student—**1** ☐ Student to teacher—**2** ☐ Student to small group—**3** ☐ Student to whole class—**4** ☐ Teacher to student—**5** ☐ Teacher to small group—**6** ☐ Teacher to whole class—**7**	**One way or two way** ☐ Student listening mostly to student—**1** ☐ Student listening mostly to teacher—**2** ☐ Student listening mostly to small group—**3** ☐ Student listening mostly to whole class—**4**	☐ Reading or writing silently—**1** ☐ Student is off task—**2**	

TIME	SPECIFIC STUDENT ACTIVITY/ LOCATION OF STUDENT FIVE-MINUTE INTERVALS	ACADEMIC SPEAKING (CHECK ONE)	ACADEMIC LISTENING ONE WAY OR TWO WAY (CHECK ONE)	STUDENT IS NOT LISTENING (CHECK ONE)	COMMENTS
		☐ Student to student—**1** ☐ Student to teacher—**2** ☐ Student to small group—**3** ☐ Student to whole class—**4** ☐ Teacher to student—**5** ☐ Teacher to small group—**6** ☐ Teacher to whole class—**7**	**One way or two way** ☐ Student listening mostly to student—**1** ☐ Student listening mostly to teacher—**2** ☐ Student listening mostly to small group—**3** ☐ Student listening mostly to whole class—**4**	☐ Reading or writing silently—**1** ☐ Student is off task—**2**	
		☐ Student to student—**1** ☐ Student to teacher—**2** ☐ Student to small group—**3** ☐ Student to whole class—**4** ☐ Teacher to student—**5** ☐ Teacher to small group—**6** ☐ Teacher to whole class—**7**	**One way or two way** ☐ Student listening mostly to student—**1** ☐ Student listening mostly to teacher—**2** ☐ Student listening mostly to small group—**3** ☐ Student listening mostly to whole class—**4**	☐ Reading or writing silently—**1** ☐ Student is off task—**2**	

online resources

Available for download from **http://resources.corwin.com/shadowingmultilinguallearners**

Norwalk-La Mirada Shadowing Multilingual Learners Sample Agenda: Half-Day Schedule

PDA 3 & 4

MLL Sample Shadowing Agenda: Half-Day Schedule

8:00—Welcome and Agenda Review

8:15—Oral/Academic Language Development Overview

10:00—Break

10:30—Listening Overview

- Shadowing Introduction/Practice With the Protocol

- Day 2 Agenda Overview/Logistics/Student Profiles

12:00—Closing

Please don't forget to wear your <u>district ID</u> to the observation school on <u>Day 2.</u>

Santa Barbara County Shadowing Multilingual Learners Sample Agenda

Day 1—Preparing for MLL shadowing

8:00—Coffee

8:30—Speaking Session

10:30—Morning Break

10:45—Listening Introduction

11:45—12:30—Lunch

12:30—Listening Continued and Practice With the Protocol

2:30—Day 2 Agenda Overview

Day 2—Meet at school sites at 8:00 a.m. (coffee at sites)

8:30—Be in classrooms by this time

8:30—10:30—Shadow MLLs in Classrooms

11:00—Back to Auditorium at Santa Barbara County Office of Education

11:00—11:30—Reflection Time

11:30—12:15—Lunch

12:15—Group Debriefing

1:15—2:30—Next Steps

- Connections to master plans and Title III plans

- Implications for professional development

Shadowing Multilingual Learners
Next Steps: Needs Assessment

On a scale of 1 through 5, with 1 being lowest and 5 being highest, which of the following areas do you consider to be the greatest need in your classroom?

1. Think-Pair-Share

1	2	3	4	5

Comments:

_____

_____

_____

_____

_____

_____

2. Teacher-Guided Reporting

Use of open-ended questions (requiring more than one-word responses)

1	2	3	4	5

Asking for linguistic clarification (grammar, specific language, etc.)

1	2	3	4	5

Encouragement

1	2	3	4	5

Recasting (restating student responses in academic language)

| 1 | 2 | 3 | 4 | 5 |

Comments:

_____

_____

_____

_____

_____

Productive Group Work (e.g., Reciprocal Teaching, Socratic Seminar, Literature Circles)

| 1 | 2 | 3 | 4 | 5 |

Comments:

_____

_____

_____

_____

_____

online resources ➤ Available for download from **http://resources.corwin.com/shadowingmultilinguallearners**

Shadowing Multilingual Learners Experience: Reflection

1. Write a short reflection on your observation of the student's learning experience.

2. Share your written experience with a partner. Identify common elements.

3. As a group of three or more, identify common elements. Select someone at your table to share common elements with the entire group.

4. Review *Looking at Classroom Talk* in Gibbons (2002), pp. 17–18.

   a. Think about your student.

   b. Think about _____ (name of student).

   c. Did you observe your student in any group work?

5. If the eight characteristics were in place within each classroom, would the observation experience have been the same?

Blank MLL Student Profile for Shadowing

- Picture of MLL for visual identification
- First name
- Date of birth
- Grade level
- Date of entry into United States
- Date of entry into district

Test Results (last three years, if possible)

Classes or Periods to Be Shadowed

PERIOD/CLASS	COURSE TITLE	TEACHER	ROOM #

ELPAC* OVERALL	LISTENING AND SPEAKING	READING	WRITING

CAASPP** FOR ELA*** AND MATH	GRADES	GPA	CAHSEE**** (HS ONLY)

*English Language Proficiency Assessments for California

**California Assessment of Student Performance and Progress

***English language arts

****California High School Exit Exam

Norwalk-La Mirada Shadowing Multilingual Learners Sample Agenda: Full-Day Schedule

PDA 3 & 4

MLL Sample Shadowing Agenda: Full-Day Schedule

8:00—Registration and Continental Breakfast

8:30—Welcome and Agenda Review

8:40—Oral Language and Development Review

10:00—Break

10:30—Listening Overview

12:00—Lunch

12:45—Shadowing Introduction/Practice With the Protocol

2:30—Day 2 Agenda Overview/Logistics/Student Profiles

3:00—Closing

Please don't forget to wear your <u>district ID</u> to the observation school on <u>Day 2.</u>

Appendix B

Academic Language Development Resources

Think-Pair-Share

OPEN-ENDED QUESTION OR PROMPT	WHAT I THOUGHT (SPEAKING)	WHAT MY PARTNER THOUGHT (LISTENING)	WHAT WE WILL SHARE (CONSENSUS)

Academic language stem for speaking: *"What I thought was . . . because . . ."*

Academic language stem for listening: *"What my partner thought was . . . because . . ."*

Academic language stem for consensus: *"What we thought was . . . because . . ."*

My Name: _____ Partner's Name: _____ Date: _____

SOURCE: Created by author, based on Lyman, F. (1981). "The responsive classroom discussion: The inclusion of all students," *Mainstreaming Digest*. University of Maryland, College Park, MD.

online resources Available for download from **http://resources.corwin.com/shadowingmultilinguallearners**

Discourse Sentence Frames for Multiple Purposes

Express an Opinion

I believe that _____ will happen because _____.

I like the story because _____.

My answer is _____ because _____.

Ask for Clarification

Can you explain what you mean?

I was wondering _____ when _____.

Summarization

The passage is mostly about _____ because _____.

Some important details are _____ and _____.

Report a Partner's Idea

My colleague suggested that _____.

_____ pointed out that _____.

Disagree

I have to kindly disagree because _____.

I had a different way of looking at this because _____.

Affirm

I appreciate your thinking because _____.

Thank you for your helping me to understand _____.

Predict

I can predict that _____ because _____.

I predict _____. The prediction is based on _____.

Paraphrase

I am understanding you to say _____ because _____.

What I'm hearing from you is _____. Is that correct?

Acknowledge Ideas

I agree with my colleague because _____.

I want to build upon my colleague's ideas _____.

Report a Group's Idea

We came to consensus on _____.

We mostly agreed, but here's where we didn't: _____.

Offer a Suggestion

I wonder if _____.

That was a good start, but how about _____.

Hold the Floor

As I was suggesting _____.

Let me think about that and get back to you.

SOURCE: Adapted from Kate Kinsella and Dutro (2010).

 Available for download from **http://resources.corwin.com/shadowingmultilinguallearners**

Partner Chant: Think-Pair-Share

Eye to eye

Knee to knee

Sit right here and learn from me

We'll speak with voices polite indeed

To share our thinking

About books we read

Our partner's thoughts can help us learn

The signal will tell us

It's time to turn.

SOURCE: Adapted by Soto (2015).

Note to Teacher: Print this in red (to stop and listen).

Listening

(*Remember to Look, Lean, and Listen.*)

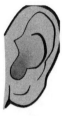

"What my partner said was . . ."

"What I'm hearing you say is . . ."

Note to Teacher: Print this in green (to go and speak).

Speaking

(*Remember to think and share your best thinking with your partner.*)

"I think/believe that . . ."

"In my opinion . . ."

IMAGE SOURCE: **pixabay.com/OpenClipart-Vectors and pixabay.com/L Mpolepy**

FRAYER MODEL—Strategy for Vocabulary Development

WORD/CONCEPT: _____

DEFINITION	ILLUSTRATION
Definition in your own words: Class definition:	

EXAMPLES	NONEXAMPLES

Reciprocal Teaching Organizer

Directions: You will assume the responsibility for helping your group to use one of four reading strategies to discuss the assigned reading: summarizing, questioning, predicting, and connecting. As you read, take notes based on your assigned strategy, and be prepared to lead a discussion for your role in your group.

SUMMARIZING	QUESTIONING	PREDICTING	CONNECTING
*Beyond retelling what happens in the reading, identify what you think are the **three most important events/details** from the reading and **explain why they are important and how they are connected.***	*Pose **at least three questions about the reading**; these could include questions that **address confusing parts of the reading** or **thought questions** that the reading makes you wonder about.*	*Identify **at least three text-related predictions**; these predictions should be based on new developments in the reading, and your predictions should help the group to **anticipate what will happen next.***	*Make **at least three connections** between ideas or events in the reading to **your own experience, the world around you**, or **other texts**. Be prepared to explain these connections to your group.*

Reciprocal Teaching Role Cards

Front

SUMMARIZER

In your own words, tell the group what the text said. Explain the reading in two or three sentences. Think like the author, and try to figure out what he or she wanted to tell you. The others in the group will help you if you get stuck or if they think you forgot something.

Back

SUMMARIZER

"Here's my summary of the most important information . . ."

Ask group members for additional input.

Front

PREDICTOR

You will tell the group what you think you will read about next. What is the writer going to say now? What will the rest of the selection be about? Tell the group what evidence in the reading leads you to believe this. The others in the group will agree or disagree with your prediction and give their own evidence.

Back

PREDICTOR

"My prediction is . . ."

"My evidence is . . ."

Ask group members if they agree or disagree and to give their evidence.

Questioner/Connector Cards

Front

QUESTIONER

You will pose three questions about the reading to the group. These could include questions that address confusing parts of the reading or thought questions that the reading makes you wonder about.

Back

QUESTIONER

"My question regarding what I was confused about . . ."

"My question regarding what I wondered about . . ."

Ask anyone else if they have questions.

Front

CONNECTOR

Make at least three connections between ideas or events in the reading to your own experience, to the world, or to other texts. Be prepared to explain these connections to your group.

Back

CONNECTOR

"My text-to-text connection was . . ."

"My text-to-life connection was . . ."

"My text-to-world connection was . . ."

Clearly explain what part of the text you are making a connection to.

Teacher-Guided Reporting Organizer

Objective: _____

Content Scenario: _____

_____

Language Scenario: _____

_____

Open-Ended Question	**Clarifying Questions**
(multiple entry points/no one-word responses)	*(linguistic, more detail, complete sentences)*
Encouragement	**Recasting**
(taking language risks)	*(restating in academic language)*

SOURCE: Adapted from Gibbons, P. (2015). *Scaffolding language, scaffolding learning: Teaching second language learners in the mainstream classroom.* Portsmouth, NH: Heinemann.

Academic Language Development Lesson Plan

Standard(s): _____

ELD Standard(s): _____

_____

Objective: _____

_____

Grade: _____ Text/textbook: _____

INTO
THROUGH
BEYOND

Expectations/Beliefs (How will students know you have high expectations?)	Linguistic Component (Contrastive analysis, standard English exposure)
SDAIE/ELD* Techniques (Visuals, manipulatives, graphic organizers, media)	**Culturally Responsive/Relevant Techniques** (Diverse texts, productive group work)

*Specially Designed Academic Instruction in English/English Language Development

The Tuning Protocol

The tuning protocol is a process for looking at a piece of curriculum and receiving feedback to incorporate into planning.

PRESENTATION: (5 MINUTES)

To begin, the presenter explains his or her work while other participants are silent.

The presenter should speak to the following:

1. Assignment or prompt that generated the student work;

2. Student learning goals for the work;

3. Samples of the work;

4. Evaluation format (scores, rubric, test);

5. Differentiation for different MLLs and skills levels.

And then . . .

6. Ask a focusing question for feedback. (Example: How can I differentiate the project? What are some interim activities? How can I teach writing skills?)

EXAMINATION OF CURRICULUM: (5 MINUTES)

Silent Examination of Paperwork Provided

Participants look at presented curriculum and take notes on where it seems to be in tune with goals and where there might be problems. Make note of warm (positive) and cool (constructive next steps around focus questions only) feedback and probing questions.

CLARIFYING QUESTIONS: (5 MINUTES)

Group members can ask clarifying questions to the presenter that have brief, factual answers. (Example: How many days is the project?)

WARM AND COOL FEEDBACK: (15 MINUTES)

Each participant shares feedback with the presenter, who is silent and taking notes. Participants identify where the work seems to meet with goals and then continue with possible disconnects and problems. They provide suggestions. Make sure to address the focus question.

REFLECTION: (5 MINUTES)

Presenter speaks to those comments and questions that he or she chooses to while participants are silent. This is not a good time to defend oneself but, rather, a time to explore interesting ideas that came out of the feedback session.

THE TUNING PROTOCOL

NOTES FOR THE PRESENTER

WARM FEEDBACK+	COOL FEEDBACK−

Questions:

online resources ↘ Available for download from **http://resources.corwin.com/shadowingmultilinguallearners**

Index

A SAGE Publishing Company

Helping educators make the greatest impact

CORWIN HAS ONE MISSION: to enhance education through intentional professional learning.

We build long-term relationships with our authors, educators, clients, and associations who partner with us to develop and continuously improve the best evidence-based practices that establish and support lifelong learning.

Solutions YOU WANT | Experts YOU TRUST | Results YOU NEED

EVENTS

>>> **INSTITUTES**

Corwin Institutes provide large regional events where educators collaborate with peers and learn from industry experts. Prepare to be recharged and motivated!

corwin.com/institutes

ON-SITE PD

>>> **ON-SITE PROFESSIONAL LEARNING**

Corwin on-site PD is delivered through high-energy keynotes, practical workshops, and custom coaching services designed to support knowledge development and implementation.

corwin.com/pd

>>> **PROFESSIONAL DEVELOPMENT RESOURCE CENTER**

The PD Resource Center provides school and district PD facilitators with the tools and resources needed to deliver effective PD.

corwin.com/pdrc

ONLINE

>>> **ADVANCE**

Designed for K–12 teachers, Advance offers a range of online learning options that can qualify for graduate-level credit and apply toward license renewal.

corwin.com/advance

Contact a PD Advisor at (800) 831-6640 or visit www.corwin.com for more information